Here are four of the greatest pitchers in baseball today:

Tom Seaver—The magician on the mound who led the New York Mets to their incredible 1969 World Series Victory; the cocky superstar who may be the finest pitcher in the major leagues. —Or does that title belong to . . .

Ferguson Jenkins—The Chicago Cubs' righthander who won the National League's 1971 Cy Young Award. Most any pitcher would be tickled pink with five consecutive twenty-game seasons, but not Fergie: "I'd like to win thirty some year, and with enough starts, I think I can."

Dave McNally—The Baltimore Orioles' "McLucky," the star lefthander who won the American League's Comeback of the Year Award in 1968, and won the openers of both the 1970 and 1971 World Series.

Mickey Lolich—The pudgy pitcher who won twenty-five games for the Detroit Tigers in 1971, and finished a very close second in the voting for the American League's Cy Young Award.

Here are stories of dreams and disappointments, struggle and success, pain and glory . . . the stories of four outstanding baseball stars.

Tom Seaver
Dave McNally
Ferguson Jenkins
Mickey Lolich

Great Pitchers Series 1

Tom Seaver
Dave McNally
Ferguson Jenkins
Mickey Lolich

By Dave Klein

Great Pitchers Series 1

TEMPO
BOOKS

GROSSET & DUNLAP
A National General Company
Publishers   New York

Copyright © 1972 by Dave Klein
ISBN: 0-448-05436-1

All Rights Reserved

Published simultaneously in Canada
Tempo Books is registered in the U. S. Patent Office
A Tempo Books Original
First Printing, March 1972

Printed in the United States of America

Contents

Tom Seaver
Dave McNally
Ferguson Jenkins
Mickey Lolich

Great Pitchers Series 1

Tom Seaver

All right, men. Who is the best pitcher in the major leagues?

"Tom Seaver," says Tom Seaver, and that's unusual.

But so, too, is Tom Seaver unusual. Besides, he is absolutely correct in his appraisal. He is, indeed, the finest pitcher in the United States.

What makes him unique is that he'll admit it. No typical athlete's act of false modesty for him. Tom Seaver is the best pitcher going and he knows it. He is most unusual. And for a twenty-seven-year-old with just five major league seasons, he is most accomplished.

To begin with, he was the main man, the catalyst, in the Miracle of 1969. That was a season in a year during which some people claim the New York Mets actually won a National League pennant and then topped it off by taking the World Series in five games from the mighty Baltimore Orioles.

But it happened. And righthander Tom Seaver was the magician on the mound who led the Mets to their improbable destiny.

Tom is a bulky, boyish, buoyant pitcher who has the uncanny ability to place a pitch precisely where he wants it, with just the right amount of speed and velocity and with all the spins, dips, twists, drops and curves other pitchers only idly imagine.

Seaver's accomplishments have been many and spectacular.

• He has won ninety-five games in his five major-league seasons, once notching twenty-five victories (1969), and twice racking up twenty (1970 and 1971).

• He holds the major-league record of nineteen strikeouts in a nine-inning game, as well as the record of ten consecutive strikeouts (same game). It was April 22, 1970, in his second starting assignment of his fourth big-league season.

• He has won a Cy Young Award, symbolic of league pitching supremacy (1969).

• He has won a Rookie of the Year Award (1967), which is a relative rarity for a pitcher. But that was the season he won sixteen games for the tenth-place team, a team which won only sixty-one.

• He has established a National League record for a righthander with 289 strikeouts in a single season, and twice in his five years he has led the league in whiffs.

• Twice he has led the National League in earned run average per game, with marks of 2.81 and 1.76, the latter a major-league high (1971) and the sixth best figure ever attained by a regular starter.

• He has been named to the National League All-Star pitching staff in each of his five seasons, and in three actual game appearances he has struck out ten batters in six innings. As a rookie, he won the game for the National League.

Furthermore, Tom Seaver has achieved superstar status, an accomplishment evidenced by, among other things, a $100,000-plus salary. He is quite certain that he has, and is, an extraordinary talent. He is convinced, but not conceited. There is a hairline difference between the terms, and it is this: Tom Seaver indulges in no self-adulation. He simply has accepted the happy fact of life that he is better and more naturally gifted than any other major-league pitcher today.

Of course, there are many outstanding pitchers. There are even a few excellent pitchers. But Tom Seaver is one of the special ones. He is the best of all the working hurlers, and by the time he retires, they just might have to give that Cy Young Award a new name.

All of which is intended to explain the jolt that stunned this sandy-haired son of sunny California in the autumn of 1971, when it was announced that the Cy Young Award had been voted not to Tom Seaver but to Ferguson Jenkins of the Chicago Cubs.

Needless to say, Tom was disappointed.

"I thought I had earned it," he said. "I had a good year, and I felt I had deserved it. But, well, I'm happy for Fergy. He's a good one."

It might be added here that the Cy Young Award is not intended to declare a man the best pitcher of his time. It is an annual honor, bestowed by the Baseball Writers Association of America on the pitcher who has had, in their opinion, the best season.

It is the feeling of a great many observers that Tom Seaver is, truly, the outstanding pitcher of today's crop, but in 1971 his season was less brilliant than Jenkins'; hence, Jenkins received the award.

The Cy Young Award is a barometer of one year's pitching. The finest hurlers of the recent past, men such as Sandy Koufax, Whitey Ford, Don Drysdale, Juan Marichal and Bob Friend, did not win it every year. But those who did hold the award for a single season were not thought to be as proficient as the clearcut stars. They were the best of the lot in a single season only.

Tom Seaver

* * *

Tom Seaver's fans, and more than a few of his non-fans, have come to call him Tom Terrific, which is not altogether proper since his first name is really George. "But I don't like George, I like Tom," says Tom. And so it is Tom.

He is the All-American Boy, a creation right out of Jack Armstrong and Superman down through Lou Gehrig and Fran Tarkenton and Paul Hornung. He is freckle-faced and light-haired, with red, rosy cheeks that tend to pudginess and a round, happy face that breaks out into a hearty, infectious laugh. He has his moments of pique; he does, at times, become upset with pressures and sportswriters and fans.

But as a pitcher, he comes very close to perfection. He is too good to be true; so good that when he loses, folks instinctively think there must be some mistake. He has no equal in the major leagues over the course of a full season, even if he does hesitate a heartbeat or two before 'fessing up to it.

There can be no doubt that Tom Seaver and the New York Mets did not just happen to each other. It was a union forged by the gods of baseball, when they finally showed mercy on the collection of men with names like Elio Chacon and Joe Moock and Choo Choo Coleman and Marv Throneberry that was called the New York Metropolitan Baseball Club, Inc.—the Mets.

It began to happen for the Mets, this change in their luck, in spring of 1965. It was June, when baseball had flowered into full bloom, when the Mets had already spent two months in their permanent summer residence, the cellar of the National League.

They needed help, desperately.

The network of circumstances had been touched off, innocently enough, six months earlier, when the Los Angeles Dodgers drafted a strong young pitcher from the University of Southern California on the fourth round of the free agent draft. His name was Tom Seaver, but he declined to accept the Dodgers' offer to turn pro. "The money," he said, "just wasn't enough," and so he decided to remain in school.

According to the rules of the baseball draft, Tom's reluctance to sign a contract made him eligible for the Phase Two draft, in which unsigned draftees can be chosen by different teams. This time it was Atlanta that picked him, and the Braves offered Tom a $50,000 contract. This time he accepted.

But disaster struck for the Braves, when the contract was ruled void by Commissioner William Eckert because U.S.C.'s season had already begun. This was a violation of baseball's agreement with the nation's colleges, but the university, at the same time, ruled

Tom ineligible for further competition because he had, after all, signed to become a professional.

Seaver was in a quandary. He correctly pointed out that he was being denied both a professional career and a collegiate one. He contacted Eckert, outlined the extent of his problem, and Eckert agreed that an injustice had been done.

By way of correction, Eckert announced that while the Braves' contract with Seaver was voided, all other teams interested in signing him could bid for his services.

There was one significant point. Those teams had to agree to at least match the offer made by the Braves.

Three teams—the Cleveland Indians, the Philadelphia Phillies and the Mets—availed themselves of this opportunity. So did the Braves.

In June, 1965, Eckert placed four slips of paper, each bearing the name of one of the teams, into a hat. Then he drew one out. It said: "New York Mets."

And somewhere up there, the immortals chuckled.

Now the Mets had a pitcher and Seaver had a home. It was Jacksonville, Fla., the Mets' highest farm team. They wanted to see what he could do, and quickly, because no team needed faster relief.

Tom spent the 1966 season with Jackson-

ville, where he won a dozen games and lost a
dozen, too. But he displayed a marvelous fastball as well as control, intelligence and determination. The Mets saw he had overwhelming potential, more of it than any rookie they
had ever before employed.

Another year would have done no good, not
for Tom and not for the Mets, and so in February of 1967 he was ordered to report to the
varsity spring training base in St. Petersburg,
Fla. The Mets knew they were going to keep
him, but they did not tell Tom. They wanted
to treat him as just another rookie.

But that was impossible. The day he put on
their uniform he became the best pitcher the
Mets had ever had, and he proved it in his first
experience against major-league hitters some
weeks later.

"It was in March, and we were playing an
exhibition game with the Minnesota Twins,"
he remembers. "I was more curious than
scared. I wanted to see the difference between
major-league and minor-league batters. I
didn't expect to make the big club but if I
did well against the Twins I knew I'd stay in
spring training with the Mets a little bit
longer."

What happened was this: In the first inning,
he fooled Ted Uhlaender on a slider and Cesar
Tovar on a curve, and both grounded out. Then
Tony Oliva (isn't he always the American
League's batting king?) sliced a double down

the left field line. Up stepped Harmon Killebrew, a sight which has been known to cause
experienced pitchers to turn into mounds of
quivering gelatin. Surely it was time for a
little case of nerves, right? Wrong.

Tom Seaver nailed the Killer.

"I decided not to get cute with him," Tom
says. "I reached back for three fastballs, and
I struck him out on those three pitches. At
that moment, I figured that maybe I could
pitch in the big leagues after all."

Tom only got better during spring training.
Pitching coach Rube Walker, who kept pinch-
ing himself to make sure he wasn't hallucinat-
ing, worked with Tom until his curve was as
efficient as his fastball, until his changeup had
the hitters swinging before the ball got to the
catcher, until he was a rookie with immense
and immediate promise.

"I remember things now," Walker says,
"that I forgot then. After we finished each
day, after we got together and talked about
the kids and the team, even after dinner, I'd
sit down and think about this boy. He had
more natural talent than any rookie I had ever
seen, and I kept thinking 'he can't be this good,
Rube, he can't be.' But he was, you know that?
He really was."

Seaver made the team, of course, and by
the time the season started he had established
himself as part of the regular rotation. On
April 20, 1967, he got his first major-league

victory when he beat the Chicago Cubs' wily veteran, Curt Simmons, 6-1.

It was the beginning.

The 1967 Mets, however, did nothing to indicate a sudden upturn in their fortunes. They were tenth again, with a 61-101 record. It was enough to force a change in managers. Wes Westrum resigned eleven games from the end of the season, and the Mets named coach Salty Parker to fill in. But no one expected he would get the job for the next season.

He didn't.

Through a series of maneuvers which can only be described as Metsicana, Gil Hodges, manager of the Washington Senators, was hired to take over for the 1968 season.

But the Mets did not actually hire Hodges. First they had to purchase him.

The confusion cropped up when the Senators complained that the Mets did not ask permission to dicker with Hodges, and since he was under contract at the time, that constituted tampering. They complained to Eckert and he saw that they were right. So the Mets, in their daffiest glory, had to buy Hodges. He came high, too—$100,000 in cash plus a young pitcher named Bill Denehy.

As a ridiculous aside, it should be mentioned that the Senators later released Denehy, who was claimed by the Mets. Then they cut him, and he finished his career with the Detroit Tigers.

Hodges had been a hometown hero long before the Mets were born. He was the powerful, home-run-hitting first baseman of the perennial champion Brooklyn Dodgers. He was an annual All-Star selection. He was as integral to the success of the team as the other stars such as Jackie Robinson, Roy Campanella, Preacher Roe, Duke Snider, Carl Furillo and Carl Erskine.

But Hodges had an image clearly his own. He was a farmboy from Indiana who arrived in the big city and never lost his simple honesty, his innocent charm, his sincere friendliness. He became as much a symbol of Brooklyn as the Dodgers, settling down in the borough, sending his children to the local schools, going into business locally.

In any case, Hodges and the Mets were together at last, and when big Gil sat down to assess his team he started with Tom Seaver.

"Best pitcher on the squad," he said. Tom had been named Rookie of the Year for his 16-13 record, 170 strikeouts, 2.76 ERA and 251 innings pitched. Of his thirteen defeats, seven were by one run. He had won seven more games, as a rookie, than anyone else on the staff, and he had convinced the rest of the league he was for real.

"I remember one game," offers Henry Aaron of the Braves, who by the end of the 1971 season needed only seventy-five home runs to pass the immortal Babe Ruth's career total of 714. "We were down by a run and I came up in the eighth inning with two men on. So what did he do. He threw me three fast ones down the pipe. I mean, really good pitches, only I couldn't get around on them. Man, I never had trouble with fastball pitchers, but this kid struck me out. He challenged me and he won. I knew right then he was gonna make a lot of trouble."

The highlight of Tom's rookie season, however, was his appearance in the All-Star game.

"I'll always remember that," he says, "because of the awe I felt at being a teammate, for a day, of guys like Aaron and Mays and Clemente. I was so nervous my knees were wobbling."

But he extracted no fear from the seasoned veterans when they saw him for the first time. "When he walked into our clubhouse he looked like some little kid from down the block," said Lou Brock, the St. Louis outfielder. "I was sure he was the bat boy, and I asked him to bring me a beer. Then he told me who he was, so I asked if his guardian knew he was up so late."

Fourteen innings later, Seaver had cause to become frazzled. The game, played in Anaheim, Calif., had gone into extra innings, and in the top of the fifteenth Cincinnati's Tony Perez broke a 1-1 tie with a home run. Walter Alston of the Los Angeles Dodgers, acting as the National League manager, called for Seaver, who was in the bullpen.

"Hold the lead, kid," he said. "It's your game."

Seaver blanched visibly.

"I remember walking across the infield," he says now, "and my knees were shaking so much I didn't know if I would make it to the mound. I just had to do something to loosen me up. As I got near second base I looked up and saw Pete Rose. I smiled at him and said: 'Hey, Pete, why don't you pitch and I'll try second, okay?' "

Rose, a veteran who is as brash as most, had to make sure of what he had heard. "I just couldn't believe the kid could be that cocky," he said. "So I asked him what he said. He repeated it. What a kid."

It accomplished what Seaver had hoped it would. "When I saw I had shocked Pete Rose," he said, "it made me feel better."

Having thus psyched himself, Seaver attacked the problems at hand ... problems with names like Tony Conigliaro, Carl Yastrzemski, Bill Freehan, Ken Berry.

Conigliaro flied to right. Yaz walked. Freehan flied to center. And Berry was struck out.

"He showed me an inside slider," Berry said. "It was as good a pitch as I could have expected, but I didn't expect it from a rookie in that kind of situation."

And so passed the rookie year, and over the

winter Seaver had time to reflect on how far he had come.

George Thomas Seaver was born on November 17, 1944, at Fresno, Calif., one of four children. His father was the prosperous owner of a raisin-packing company. Mr. Seaver had been an outstanding athlete in his own right, and a member of the U.S. Walker Cup golf team in the mid-1930's.

"I wasn't sure about my future," Tom recalls, "I didn't know what I wanted to do, so after I graduated from Fresno High I went to work in my dad's company, loading crates for two bucks an hour. It was the first job I had had, and six months later I joined the Marines. That was the smartest thing I ever did.

"I worked hard and my weight increased from one-sixty-five to one-eighty-five. I matured mentally and philosophically, and when I was discharged I knew I needed a college education. I thought I might want to be a dentist, but I wasn't sure. I just knew I wanted to go to college."

Tom enrolled at Fresno City College, and when his pitching attracted attention, he was offered a scholarship by U.S.C., which he accepted. "I had decided to play one year at U.S.C. and then sign a pro contract and finish school in the off-season," Tom says, "and that's just how it worked out."

In the summer of 1964 and the spring of 1965, Tom pitched for a semi-pro team in

Alaska, the Goldpanners. "It really helped," he said. "The sun shines all the time there in the summer, so it made my fastball tough to hit. No one could see it."

The 1968 season brought Seaver and Hodges together, and it became a relationship of mutual respect. "I could see he was a good manager," Seaver said. "He knew what he was doing. He could be quiet and patient and easy-going. But cross him once and he gets tough. He knows what he wants, and he'll treat you like a man as long as you don't take advantage of him."

For his part, Hodges found Seaver too good to be true. "He was just a kid, but he was mature beyond his years. I knew how much talent he had, but I couldn't believe his maturity. I knew he'd be my team leader, and I knew he'd be the pitcher everyone said he would be. He wanted it badly enough to work for it. It's a treat to have worked with him."

Hodges had been busy since taking the Mets' job. He found new faces to insert into the line-up. He brought up Cleon Jones from the farm in Buffalo and Cleon's bat began exploding. He traded to get centerfielder Tommie Agee from the White Sox. He put a rookie named Ken Boswell at second base and another named Bud Harrelson at shortstop.

Jerry Grote, in his third major-league year, had just begun to develop into an All-Star catcher. Ron Swoboda was a promising rookie outfielder with a powerful bat, and the pitching staff which already boasted Seaver was enriched by two more rookie marvels—Jerry Koosman and Nolan Ryan.

In all, Hodges had forged a competitive team, although no one was ready to believe it yet. There were still too many good loser jokes to go around. ("Hear about the Met who caught a cold? He dropped it.")

Hodges was optimistic in spring training, a strange condition for a man managing the Mets. But he was sincere in his belief that the team would improve. He proved to be right.

The fact that the Mets finished ninth—a step up, but hardly worth a celebration— masked two vitally important facts: They had won more games than ever before in their history, seventy-three; and they had finished just eight games short of a .500 season, which for them would have been super-sensational.

It was there for all to see, but no one looked hard enough to find it. The Mets were moving up.

Seaver won sixteen games again, lost twelve and finished with a 2.20 ERA, 205 strikeouts, seven shutouts and 278 innings pitched. He had established himself as a quality performer. Superstardom was a step away.

Koosman was even better. He finished 19-12, missing his final two attempts at becoming the Mets' first-ever twenty-game winner (but they had had six pitchers who lost twenty or more in previous years). He added 178 strike-outs and, with seven shutouts, tied a major league record for rookies.

Ryan, with a Bob Feller fastball ("better," says Hodges) and absolutely no control, won six and lost nine. On the days when he was able to locate the plate, his hummer added up to 133 strikeouts in 134 innings, but he walked seventy-five and scared the hell out of the opposing hitters.

"He's so fast," says Pete Rose, "that you think about what could happen if that fastball ever got away from him. You have to be a little more careful, a little more cautious. He's frightening."

With the season concluded, Hodges declared that he was pleased. "Not that I'm happy with ninth place," he explained, "but we showed improvement at almost every position. We can win even more games next season. Even eighty."

When he next repeated that goal, it was during spring training of 1969, and the group of reporters to whom he was speaking shook their heads in disbelief. They were, for the most part, veterans of the Mets' impossible years, and they held out no chance at all, not even for respectability.

One of them muttered: "If they can win eighty, how many more would they need to . . . to . . . no, it's preposterous."

But Hodges was serious, and when he became annoyed at the ridiculing which went on in the metropolitan area newspapers, he made sure to repeat his statement. "You know," he said, "I'm tempted to say we could win the pennant, but I know that would sound foolish. But look at it. We're in division play this year. We have six teams in our division. If we can stay with the Cubs and the Cards, we can be in it, because I'm sure we can beat the rest (Pittsburgh, Philadelphia and Montreal)."

And 1969 did become the Year of the Miracle, a year which catapulted Tom Seaver to star status. Seldom had any pitcher before him put it together in quite so devastating a performance.

Tom finished the season with a 25-7 record, a 2.21 ERA, 208 strikeouts and 272 innings worked. He led the league in victories and in winning percentage (.781). He won his last ten starts, he didn't lose after August 5 and he brought home six critical victories during the crucible-heat pressure of the September stretch run.

He was a unanimous choice for the Cy Young Award. He was the year's number one celebrity.

The peak of his season, individually, was his game against the contending Cubs on July 9. Chicago, which occupied first place for most of the season, came to New York's Shea Stadium for a crucial four-game series. The Mets, however unlikely, were in second place, four games behind the Cubs and secure there, since St. Louis, in third, trailed by eleven and a half.

The Shea Stadium fans, perhaps baseball's most loyal, had been stricken with pennant fever, even in July, and they filled the seats for this one. There were 59,083 of them in attendance that night, and they seemed to be sitting in the aisles and along the outfield grass.

"I have been to every game in the history of the Mets," intoned radio-TV announcer Lindsay Nelson to the millions who could not buy a ticket, "and I have never seen anything like this night. People are everywhere, and there is an electricity in the air over Shea Stadium."

The Mets took an early lead, and the crowd got out of hand. In the first inning special police had to remove half a dozen fans from the black background screen in centerfield, the so-called "batter's eye," which prevents the ball from being lost to the hitter in a sea of white shirts.

Seaver had never been as good. The Mets built their lead to 4-0, and it was the top of the ninth inning. No Cub had gotten a hit. No Cub had drawn a walk. No Cub had reached base on an error or a balk or a passed ball. In other words, Tom Seaver was three outs removed from a rare perfect game.

"I remember hoping no one would hit the

23

ball to me," said third baseman Wayne Garrett, then a rookie. "I was scared to death I'd mess up the play."

Seaver bent to his task with almost hypnotic concentration. He remembers the feeling of the moment, "and I always will," he says, "because it's never been quite like that since. My arm felt so light, just like a feather. I felt ten feet tall. My heart was beating so fast I could just feel the adrenalin going into my system."

Catcher Randy Hundley was first up, and on orders from Cubs' manager Leo Durocher, he tried to bunt. It was a rather ungentlemanly move, but he tapped the ball too hard, too close to the mound, and Seaver pounced on it. "He really did me a favor," Tom said later.

Catcher Jerry Grote screamed at Seaver as he fielded the nubber. "Take your time," he pleaded, "please take your time."

Seaver threw Hundley out.

Now it was a rookie named Jimmy Qualls, who was batting .243 for the season. He was a sharp pull hitter, and Grote, going with Seaver's best pitch of the night, called for a fastball. It came in waist-high, too good. Qualls swung and the ball was punched into the left-center alley, where Agee and Jones both broke for it. They converged, but not in time. The ball fell between them, a clean single. Qualls stood on first as the crowd hushed in an eerie silence. Then they went wild, cheering for their hero, who had been denied his once-in-a-lifetime chance.

"I was numb," Seaver said later. "I could have had it. You just don't get another chance like that. I can't really measure the disappointment I felt, not even now."

Seaver finished the game with a one-hit shutout, a game in which he struck out eleven and moved the Mets to within three games of the Cubs—and first place.

But the fans were still chanting for Seaver after the game, while he was in the clubhouse talking about his near-miss with destiny. "It was an exceptional fastball he had," Grote was saying. "Listen, when you can throw a fastball right down the middle past Billy Williams you really have a hummer, because Williams has the quickest bat in the league. Qualls was new to us. We'd never seen him before so we just felt him out. His first time up he got one down the middle and hit it deep to right, but Tom threw only a couple down the middle all night."

Seaver, standing on a trainer's table in the center of the locker room to accomodate the mass of newsmen, radio and TV workers and team officials, admitted to deep disappointment.

"We won," he said, "and we're going to win this pennant. But I do feel bad about the perfect game. We are going to be winners. I've said that all along. This lovable loser stuff isn't funny anymore, not to me and not to the rest of the team. But I sure do hate to see that perfect game get away.

"When I walked off the field after the game, I saw my wife Nancy in her seat near home plate. She was crying. That's when I smiled. I said to her 'look, a one-hitter isn't so bad, is it?' We both laughed.

"But let me tell you something. When I came to bat in the eighth inning, those fans were super. There was a roar like I have never heard before. It was deafening, almost scarey. I took my time and the umpire didn't hurry me. I was really trying to get it [the perfect game] for the fans, too."

Seaver's superseason of 1969 was over; the Mets had won the N.L.'s Eastern Division pennant by eight games over the crumbled Cubs, whom they destroyed later in another head-to-head set, and now they were to start the best-of-five series with Atlanta, the Western Division winner.

Tom started the first game and won. The Mets won the next two as well. The Braves never had a chance, and they should have known better than to try to stand in the way of a miracle picking up momentum.

The impossible dream had become a highly implausible, but recognized, reality. There they were, the lowly New York Mets, in a World Series against the juggernaut from Baltimore, the American League champion

Orioles, who had swept their series from the Minnesota Twins.

Naturally, the Mets lost the first game, and the sportswriters of the country nodded their heads in I-told-you-so certainty. Naturally the Mets won the next four, including a ten-inning, 2-1 Seaver victory in the fourth game of the Series, a six-hitter.

It was the most significant game of the Series. The Mets held a 2-1 edge in games, but should the Orioles win and tie it up, the advantage would have been sacrificed and it would have meant going back to Baltimore, something the Mets did not want to do.

"I knew all those things when the game started," Tom said. "I had never been in a more important game in my life. I realized how much we had accomplished, but how little it would have meant if we couldn't finish it off. I never wanted to win a game as much in my life."

He won ... the Mets won ... they went on to shatter the Orioles' egos and the fans tore up the field in celebration when it was official. It took months for the sod to grow back, sad news for the winter tenants of Shea, the N.F.L.'s New York Jets.

There was little else for Tom Seaver to conquer. He had won twenty-five games and the Cy Young Award. Indeed, he finished a close second to San Francisco's Willie McCovey in the Most Valuable Player voting. He had fame and fortune and following. He and Nancy were pursued by advertising men, by sponsors for televison commercials. The money flowed, the winter was good and the world was never better for a young pitcher.

And in 1970, at least early in the season, it got even better.

On April 22, Seaver started against the San Diego Padres. Again, it was one of those extraordinary days in which the fastball had a life of its own and the curve dropped down on hitters like a hammer. The Padres couldn't touch him.

Strikeout followed strikeout and the fans became aware of a special excitement. They were buzzing, trying to find out just how many strikeouts Seaver had.

Finally, the ultra-modern scoreboard in rightfield flashed its message: "Tom Seaver has nine strikeouts," it read. It was the top of the sixth inning, and two were out. But no sooner had the lights appeared then they had to be extinguished, for Tom made it ten to close out the sixth, fanning hard-hitting Al Ferrara.

The major-league record for a nine-inning day game was eighteen strikeouts, set by Bob Feller of Cleveland in 1938. Steve Carlton of St. Louis had struck out nineteen in a night game in 1969, but night lights work to a pitcher's advantage. Baseball is still a game meant to be played by day.

Tom had his chance. He had three innings left, nine outs to achieve. If he could strike out all nine men, he would have his record. It did not seem possible; but then, nothing this wunderkind has done seemed possible until he did it.

The seventh inning came and down went Nate Colbert, Dave Campbell and Jerry Morales. "He had perfect stuff," Grote said. "Zoom, zoom, zoom; fastball, slider, curve. They couldn't come close to him. I just wonder if any pitcher has ever been better."

That made it thirteen strikeouts, and four in a row. In the eighth inning three more Padres—Bob Barton, Ramon Webster and Ivan Murrell—fanned. That made it sixteen for the game, and seven straight. With seven in a row, Tom had tied a major league record held by six others, and now the ninth inning came and with it all the drama any fan could expect to find in a baseball stadium.

Van Kelly led off the ninth. He whiffed. Now it was Clarence Gaston, and he went down swinging. Tom had eighteen, and nine straight. It was down to the final out, and up stepped Ferrara, a power hitter who in the second inning had homered for the Padres' only run. But the Mets had managed just two runs, and with the score 2-1, not only the records but the game itself was on the line.

"I decided I wasn't going to lose this chance, too," Tom recalled. "I just let the fastball rip."

Ferrara acknowledged the challenge. "I knew what was coming," he said, "because it was his best shot against mine. He won it. I almost didn't see the third strike."

"I only tried for two in that game intentionally," Seaver said. "They were the sixteenth [which broke Ryan's team record] and the last one. I went after only those two. I must admit I felt a sense of accomplishment after that, of having further proved myself as a major league pitcher."

It appeared as though the Mets were on their way to another pennant, but Tom suffered through an extended period of being just good, not great. The team didn't score many runs for him, and while he won fourteen of his first eighteen starts, he captured only four of his final twelve. He finished 18-12, and he led the league in strikeouts (283) and ERA (2.81).

But he had won only once in the team's final fifty games, and without Tom to take them through, the Mets faltered. Seaver was annoyed, both with himself and with Hodges, for pitching with only three days' rest.

"I'm not at my strongest when I go every fourth day," he said. "I have a schedule all worked out. I need four days between starts. I have to sleep twelve hours two days before I pitch and then ten hours the day before. It's my way, and I'm going to insist on it. I'm no value to the team if I'm not at my best."

So in 1971 he worked with four days' rest, only twice going with three, and on the final day of the season he won his twentieth game. His 1.76 ERA led the major leagues, and his 289 strikeouts established a National League record for right-handed pitchers in a season. He had twenty-one complete games in his thirty-five starts, a tribute to his durability and stamina.

But he couldn't do it all. Other problems kept the Mets from the pennant again.

What lies ahead now for Tom Seaver?

Hodges, for one, feels his future is limitless. "He can do anything he wants to," says his manager. "He is the most complete pitcher in the majors. He has all the pitches, the control, the intelligence. He knows all the hitters' weaknesses. He is strong and durable, and smart as a whip. Also, he's not afraid of anyone. That's important for a pitcher. They have to be a little bit arrogant.

"I've seen him challenge the best hitters in the league, the guys like Aaron and McCovey and Clemente and Mays, and he beats them. They can't hit him when he knows he has to put one pitch past them. He's sure to stay at the top for years to come, and if he doesn't win twenty games every season, or damn close to it, I'll be surprised."

So the Cy Young Award which eluded Tom in 1971 should be back in his portfolio soon, if Hodges is right. Seaver is too good to miss out many more times, and even without the annual award, he is generally acknowledged as the finest pitcher in the major leagues.

The fact that the Mets are no longer the jokes of the National League is already quite established; the fact that their transition from clowns to professional craftsmen is closely tied to Tom Seaver's acquisition is hardly coincidental.

Cy Young or not, Tom Seaver is the best there is.

Ferguson Jenkins

The question: What do John Herrnstein, Adolfo Phillips, Bob Buhl and Larry Jackson all have in common?

The answer: They are the men responsible for bringing Ferguson Jenkins to the Chicago Cubs, since they were the other four major-league players involved in the historic five-man trade made with the Philadelphia Phillies on April 21, 1966.

John Holland, the general manager of the Cubs, would have known the answer in an instant, as well as the precise date. He has good reason to remember the trade, since it was the best deal he ever made for the Cubs.

Phillips, an outfielder, and Herrnstein, a first baseman, were wrapped up in gift paper along with Jenkins and sent to Chicago in return for Buhl and Jackson, two veteran pitchers.

It worked out sensationally well for Chicago. "I wish I could make a trade like that once a year," Holland smiles. "Fergie is the best pitcher in the major leagues today."

Holland has every right to his opinion, and certainly there are many who would agree with him. But in the context of the full complement of pitchers eligible for such a distinction, no one seems to come closer than Tom Seaver of the New York Mets.

Seaver has emerged as the talent-laden pitcher of the major leagues, a more natural talent than Jenkins. But Jenkins has proven to be consistent, as a winner and as a strikeout artist.

Since that switching of uniforms and shifting of allegiance, Jenkins has showed himself to be a superstar righthander, perhaps not the best in the league but certainly close to it, and equally consistent.

Still, at this relatively early stage in both their careers, it might be premature to select one as the unequivocal best. They are both superb, Seaver and Jenkins.

Jenkins, a 6-5, 205-pounder, has won twenty or more games each year for the last five seasons, and at the conclusion of the 1971 season he was named recipient of the Cy Young Award, which represents pitching excellence for a given season. Seaver was close, and many

felt he should have won it. But Fergy was the winner, and an equal number of fans felt it was an honor long overdue.

"Who am I to say no?" Fergie laughed when told of the award. His words were guaranteed to bring a smile to his lips, since he has used them at every turning point in his baseball career.

He said them first in Ontario, when he was fifteen years old and a scout for the Phillies, Tony Lucadello, told him he was a pretty fair first baseman but that the fastest way for him to reach the major leagues was as a pitcher. He strongly recommended that Ferguson learn how to pitch, and said the Phillies would be more than interested in signing him if he showed any promise at all on the mound.

"Who am I to say no?" Jenkins reasoned, and so he proceeded to learn the art of putting the ball where it cannot be hit. He also took to heart another of Lucadello's suggestions, which was for him to spend the year chopping wood in order to strengthen his shoulders. "I must have chopped down half the trees in Canada," he laughs.

The phrase was uttered again when Fergie was with a Winter League team in Puerto Rico and the manager, Cal McLish, asked him to think about switching to relief work, saying he did not feel Fergie could cut it in the major leagues as a starter. Since McLish was a former major-league pitcher, Jenkins readily agreed. "Who am I to say no?" he said, and he went about becoming a relief pitcher.

Then, after he had made it to the Phillies' roster, at a time when he had become the second most important man in the Phillies' bullpen, he was told by team owner Robert Carpenter that he was going to the Chicago Cubs.

"We need experienced players," Carpenter said. "They asked for you, and we made the trade."

Fergie smiled resignedly. "Who am I to say no?" he said, as he packed his bags.

The same words came up again during mid-season of 1966, when Leo Durocher, the manager of the Cubs, told him he was going to be a starter again. Leo said he had too much talent to waste it in the bullpen.

"Who," Fergie said, "am I to say no?" And he went on to register a 20-13 record the following season.

It has been five years since then, and Ferguson Jenkins has been the only National Leaguer since 1960 to register twenty victories in five consecutive seasons. He has also led the league in strikeouts (273 in 1969), in victories (24 in 1971) and in fewest earned runs allowed (118 in 1970). He is the reason why the Cubs have come so close to so many pennants year after year, but he is by no means the reason why they have failed to cash in on all their promise even once.

He is, by anyone's standards, a superstar.

* * *

Ferguson Arthur Jenkins was born on December 13, 1943, in Chatham, Ontario. He always wanted to be a baseball player in the major leagues of the United States, a rather unusual desire among Canadian-born youngsters, who usually grow up playing hockey and to whom the players on the Montreal Canadiens and the Toronto Maple Leafs are national heroes.

"I know there weren't many Canadian baseball players," he says, "because most of the kids up there go to hockey right away. Well, I tried it, and I liked it. And I liked basketball, too. But what I loved was baseball. It was what I really wanted to do."

So by the time he was fifteen, Jenkins was an accomplished high-school and summer-league player, a first baseman who hit towering home runs. He hit so many of them, so often, that the Phillies sent Lucadello scurrying past customs to investigate this Canadian giant.

That's when Lucadello decided that as a first baseman, Fergie would make a wonderful pitcher.

Jenkins, ever agreeable, said goodbye to hockey and goodbye to basketball (although he did tour Canada with the Harlem Globetrotters in 1968) and concentrated on becoming a pitcher.

"I was always able to throw the ball fast enough," he says, "but I had no idea of what a pitcher must do. I just stood out there and reared back and threw as hard as I could. When you're sixteen and seventeen you can look pretty good with just a fastball."

The scouts came flocking back, but Jenkins remembered Tony Lucadello and signed with the Phillies in 1962.

"He must have been pleased with my progress," Jenkins says. "As for me, I thought I was ready to pitch in the majors. But I soon found out I had a lot to learn."

It did not seem that way, however, when the Phillies sent him to their Miami team in the Florida State League. He took the league apart, and by mid-season he was 7-2 with sixty-nine strikeouts in sixty-five innings and an incredible 0.97 ERA.

So, in order to find out quickly what sort of find they had made, the Phillies jumped Jenkins all the way up to Triple-A minor-league baseball, to Buffalo of the International League. He earned a 1-1 record there, and gained valuable experience facing the better batters.

The following season he started with Arkansas in the International League, but ran into difficulty and was 0-1 when the Phillies shipped him back to Miami. There he regained his confidence and his rhythm, and he finished with a 12-5 record, striking out 135 men in 140 innings.

During the next two years, he made minor-league stops in Chattanooga (Tenn.) of the Southern League and again with Arkansas, which by that time had been realigned as part of the Eastern Division of the Pacific Coast League. He was on his way up; a big, gangly kid with smoke on his fastball and a talent for pinpoint control.

It was in the winter of 1965 that he accepted McLish's decision and took up relief pitching, and when the season closed that summer the Phillies brought Fergie up to the major-league roster for the final few weeks of the schedule. He reported in September and pitched a dozen strong innings of relief, emerging with a 2-1 record and a satisfactory 2.25 ERA.

It was a strong enough performance for him to draw praise from the Phillies, along with the promise that he would be their number one man in the bullpen in 1966. But that December, back home with his parents in Ontario, he read that the team had obtained Darold Knowles, a seasoned reliever, in a trade with the Baltimore Orioles.

"I was very disappointed at first," Jenkins says now, "but after a while I tried to accept what had happened. I was just a rookie and they [the Phillies] couldn't possibly know for sure how I would stand up over a full season.

43

Knowles was a top man, and I think the bull-pen is as important as any area of a team. I began to see the logic in their move. I understood why they wouldn't want to go into a season with an untested kid as their top relief man. After I thought it through, I accepted it. I honestly felt I would be satisfied if I became the number two relief man behind Knowles. Besides, who was I to say no?"

So in February of 1966 Fergie reported to spring training with the Phillies content in the direction his career was going. "I was only twenty-three years old and I was going to be the second man in a major league bullpen," he says. "I thought that was pretty good, you know?"

But another man figured Ferguson Jenkins was even better than that; too good to be with another team. He was John Holland, the man who engineered the trade.

"At the time, everybody figured the player we really wanted was Phillips," Holland says, "and we did want him, of course. We felt he was a fine young outfielder who could hit and field and run. He had great promise. But we wanted Jenkins, too. We had been following his minor-league career, as we did with all young players, and we saw potential in him. Maybe we didn't think of him as a super starter right away, but we knew we wanted him.

"We knew, also, that the Philadelphia team

needed some veteran pitchers. At the same time, we were in a rebuilding program. We wanted as many promising youngsters as we could get, and it suited our needs to make room on the roster by trading the older men. The Phillies wanted Buhl [he was to go 6-8 in two seasons with them] and Jackson. We went for youth, and the Phillies took our veterans. At the time it was a deal which pleased both teams."

But now, with Jackson and Buhl long since gone, the Phillies must often gnash their teeth in disappointment as they watch Jenkins reel off victories. While the loss of Herrnstein and Phillips did not hurt them much, they have developed one glaring weakness lately—the lack of a solid, consistent, workhorse starting pitcher.

The day after the trade was made, Fergie was standing in the sunshine in Wrigley Field, shagging flies, when Durocher walked up to him.

"What do you want to do on this ball club?" he asked.

"I'd like to be a relief pitcher," Jenkins replied, since he had already been told relief work was his best avenue to stardom.

"I was shocked," Leo said later, "because most young pitchers are just itching to start. They think older guys wind up as the bullpen pitchers. They all think they have enough talent to start. I was surprised, but I didn't

45

want to upset the kid by making him adjust to something new so quickly, and so I agreed with him."

Jenkins, too, remembers the incident. "I think I stunned him," he smiles. "I don't think he was able to believe what he heard. But what did I know? Everybody had always told me I was going to make it as a reliever."

Durocher went along with Fergie's wishes, using him mostly as a late-inning relief specialist. But by the end of August his record was 2-6, "although I wasn't all that bad," Jenkins says. "Still, I knew it wasn't making the Cubs very happy, and I was disappointed in myself."

It was then that Durocher put his foot down and made up his mind to effect a change.

"Every time I gave him the ball he was getting the batters out," Leo remembers. "He was blanking teams for four, five innings, striking out the big hitters, scaring everybody with his beautiful fastball. He seemed strong enough to do anything, and I guess if I left him alone he would have developed into a pretty good relief man.

"But I decided against it, because my starters weren't setting any records. 'Hell, I'm getting tired of this nonsense,' I said. 'If he can throw like that, he's going to get out there and do it for nine innings.'"

Again, Leo was careful not to jolt Jenkins with the news.

"I suspected he might get nervous if I told him he would be starting in four days," Leo recalls, "so I didn't say anything at all to him. I just sat him down in the bullpen, and I left orders that he was not to even warm up. When he didn't get into a game for three days, he got curious as to why I wasn't using him, and I guess he was a little concerned, too. But I figured it was a good way to get him angry. Good pitchers have to be a little angry, you know.

"Then, on the fourth day, we all showed up at the park before a game and I just handed him the ball and told him he was my starter. Just think. Here I had a kid with all this ability and talent and I had to con him into starting."

Fergie doesn't see it that way. "I would have been more at ease if he told me," he says. "I don't think it would have upset me."

That first start came against the Mets, and Fergie went nine full innings before leaving with the game tied. He won his next start—against the Phillies, incidentally—and finished the season with three victories in five outings to push his final record to 6-8.

Now he was a starter with a future, and even Fergie saw that the change had been a blessing.

"Once I began to win as a starter, I enjoyed the idea," he says. "I just couldn't wait for spring training. I was so excited about the way the season finished I was ready to start all over again the next day."

Jenkins had even more reason to be excited about spring training of 1967, as he discovered when he reported to the team's base in Arizona.

Durocher had hired a new pitching coach, Joe Becker, who had filled a similar position with St. Louis the season before. These two men were to establish a mutually beneficial relationship.

"I had noticed Fergy during the tail end of the sixty-six season," Becker said, "but that wasn't so smart on my part. Heck, we had all been impressed with the way he came on as a starter. He was just brimming over with natural talent, but he was tipping off his pitches. I had noticed that much.

"We worked all spring on masking his pitches, on hiding them in the motion of his delivery. He never realized what he was doing wrong, but a veteran player or a coach could have spotted it right off. They could tell when he was coming with the fastball, the curve, even the changeup. When he learned to hide the ball and to cut down on his big windup, he became smoother and I think he became twice as effective."

As spring training camps go, Fergie had a doozy. "They couldn't touch him," Becker crowed.

In one game he struck out six straight batters, and they said they couldn't even see his fastball. It was his first season as a regular rotation pitcher, and he was already the star of the staff. He was so powerful all spring the Cubs had no trouble choosing their Opening Day starter. There really was no choice; Fergie had earned it all spring.

The Cubs were to open with the Phillies, and on the mound for Philadelphia was veteran Jim Bunning, a man with two no-hitters, one a perfect game, to his credit, and a man who stands second only to Walter Johnson in all-time career strikeouts.

Jenkins won the game, 4-2, allowing only five hits, and he went on to win his first three starts of the season. But then he lost his next three, and he grew depressed and uncertain.

Becker had to step in and help.

"He was still too inexperienced to know that slumps just happen, that they come and go," Becker explained. "We had to cheer him up. More important, we had to find something he could work on, something he could change to get his mind off the losses. We decided he could use more warmup time before starts, so he tried that and it worked."

It worked so well that Fergie won eight of his next ten games and was 11-5 by mid-season. That earned him a spot on the National League All-Star team. In the clubhouse before the game, manager Walt Alston spoke to the players. Then he said: "Jenkins will pitch the middle three innings."

"I was so surprised I almost fell off my stool," Fergie laughs, "and when my turn came, I was scared to death. But I got out there, and when I started humming the fast one, I felt more confident. I know I was only scheduled for three innings, but I was kind of disappointed when I left the game. I was really grooving out there."

In his three-inning stint, Jenkins struck out six batters. But he was touched for the American League's only run in the fifteen-inning contest, which was won by the National League (and Tom Seaver), 2-1. Yet the home run ball he served up to Baltimore's Brooks Robinson was more than atoned for by his dazzling strikeout performance, which victimized such feared hitters as Mickey Mantle, Tony Oliva, Harmon Killebrew, Rod Carew, Tony Conigliaro and Jim Fregosi.

Jenkins returned to the Cubs and finished with a 9-8 mark for the second half of the season, enough to earn for him his first twenty-victory distinction. He won No. 20 on the final day of the season, beating Cincinnati, 4-1, and clinching third place for the Cubs. It was their highest finish in several years.

Toward the end of the season, Jenkins ran into an injury serious enough to threaten his chance of winning the twenty games.

In the middle of August, in a game against

the Phillies, he bent over to start his windup and pain shot through him. He could not straighten up, and he admitted that he had nearly passed out from the series of sharp stabs which ran down his back and into his legs.

He was carried off the field in that half-upright position, but when the trainer was able to pop his back into place, he refused to leave the game. He went back out and pitched four more innings, finally leaving after the ninth with the score tied.

"The doctors took X-rays, and found I had been born missing one vertebra in my lower back," he explains. "They told me I'd be one or two inches taller if it was there. I never knew it, because I had never been bothered by it before. They said there was nothing they could do about it, that it was something I'd just have to learn to live with. The biggest thing is the pain. Sometimes it's really bad."

As a result, Jenkins has to take muscle-relaxing pills before he pitches, and some mornings he wakes up with stabbing pains. When he has to pitch on those days, the pain causes him to assume an odd, stiff-backed stance on the mound.

But the 1967 season had come as a revelation to Jenkins and the Cubs, and Fergie credits Becker for his success—and his continued success. Becker is retired now, but Jenkins feels he owes him a debt of gratitude.

"When Joe joined the club, he told me he was going to help me make a million dollars," Fergie says. "Then he listed four things I had to do.

"He said I had to work hard, concentrate, make the batter hit my pitch and be ready to go out and throw hard ever fourth day. Where he helped me technically was getting me to cut down on my big windup, and getting me to study movies of myself taken during games. I've been amazed, and so have the other guys here, at how much you can pick up on your mistakes by seeing yourself on film."

Another problem Jenkins has had to control is his tendency to "relax."

"I wouldn't call it laziness," says Cubs catcher Randy Hundley, "but Fergie's the kind to take things easy. Like before he's supposed to warm up, he won't be half dressed. And when he's pitching he'll get careless. He'll get a good hitter out easily and then hang a slider around the letters for an ordinary guy and boom, home run. He isn't concentrating all the time. Joe [Becker] and I would holler at him to bend his back. Sometimes he'd be standing straight up when he pitched, and they'd hit home runs off those high ones. I'll have to say this about him, though: Fergie will listen to you. I'd chew him out and he'd nod his head, kind of sadly, and say: 'You're right, you're right.' Other guys, you can chew them out and they get mad at you."

Jenkins agrees. "I hate to admit it, but I do let up sometimes. It's subconscious, I guess, when I relax out there. A good kick in the pants sure helps. Now I work to keep myself sharp mentally, too. I have a tendency to take things too easy, and I know it hurts me sometimes. I have to work hard to make sure it doesn't happen, but sometimes I forget myself and then I get burned."

After his big season of 1967, everyone knew Fergie had arrived as a major-league starter. His succeeding years only proved it. He was 20-15 in 1968, 21-15 in 1969, 22-16 in 1970 and 24-13 in 1971, his Cy Young season.

In each year he has been well over the 200 mark in strikeouts—236, 260, 273, 274 and 263—while at the same time he has kept his bases-on-balls total down to an enviable minimum—83, 65, 71, 60 and 37. When looked at in the light of innings pitched, those walks become even more admirable. In his five straight twenty-plus seasons, he has worked in 289, 308, 311, 313 and 325 innings, the 1971 total enough to lead the league.

His 1971 season, although it failed to turn up a pennant for the Cubs, points up just how effective he has become. His totals for the year enabled him to lead the league not only in victories and innings-pitched but in complete games, thirty, and his 2.67 ERA was among the league's top five figures.

For much of the season, the Cubs were involved in a race for the National League's Eastern Division pennant with Pittsburgh—the ultimate winner—St. Louis and New York. Down the stretch, no pitcher was more effective, or more frequently worked, than Fergie.

By the end of August, a Chicago rally had taken them to only three games behind the Pirates in the loss column, and the Cubs were making all the right moves in their bid to overtake the leaders.

"This year it's going to be different," he said at the time, although he was not to be proven correct. It was the day he won his twentieth game, a 3-2 victory over Houston, to become the first twenty-game winner in the league and the first man to win that many for five straight seasons since Warren Spahn accomplished the feat from 1956 through 1960.

"We're hungrier now," he said, "and we won't tire out. I think we have enough momentum to win it now."

Indeed, the Cubs had trailed Pittsburgh by eleven and a half games just a month earlier, and at the end of the season it was Chicago that supplied all the pressure on the Pirates.

Most of that pressure came from the Chicago pitching staff, and it was led, of course, by Jenkins. The day he won his twentieth game he also notched his twenty-fourth complete game in thirty starts. For a former relief pitcher, he sure wasn't giving his one-time colleagues much work.

The rest of the players in the National League agree that 1971 marked Fergie's best season in baseball. He was working quickly, smoothly, apparently having established a private rhythm with his stance, windup, delivery and pitch selection. "His control was fantastic," says Hundley. "I remember one stretch when he had walked just twenty-seven guys in more than two hundred and fifty innings, and only seven in the last one hundred."

Jenkins agreed that it had been his best season, but he added that "it ended up with another disappointment. We wanted to win the pennant badly. It would have made all the hard work worthwhile. But we just couldn't keep up the pressure. We had the Pirates running, and then we let them get ahead again. There weren't enough games left for us to recoup again. The season was too far gone.

"Personally, it was a good season for me. But I don't like to consider the individual record; it's the team that really matters, and when you don't come in first, the team doesn't accomplish what it set out to do way back in spring training. The object is to win, to win more than any other team. We didn't do it, and so the season for us came up short."

In one outstanding effort, Jenkins came face to face with the Atlanta Braves' Henry Aaron, who needs only seventy-five more home runs to surpass the immortal Babe Ruth's career total of 714. Henry had come to Chicago with a twenty-two-game hitting streak; he went zero-for-five, fanning three times.

"I could have stayed at bat all day and I wouldn't have got a hit off him," Aaron said. "That day, he was the best pitcher I faced all season. I don't think there are any better in the league. I wouldn't put him second to anyone, but I'd bunch maybe four at the top, guys like Seaver and Jenkins and Marichal and Gibson. They're all quality pitchers, and the best in our league."

As an individual, Jenkins has specific thoughts about fame and success, and money.

"I've never been a very fast-living kind of guy," he says, "so perhaps I don't get as much publicity or attention as some of the others. It bugs me sometime. You know, all you read about are guys like Seaver and Marichal and Gibson. Maybe I live slower than they do, and for that reason maybe I don't get the attention they do. But I like money as much as anyone, and now maybe the promotional end of the income will begin to come my way."

Financially, Fergie is assured of a $100,000-plus contract for 1972. He earned "in the neighborhood" of $90,000 in 1971, and says the Cy Young Award and the fifth straight twenty-game season should take him over the top. The exact amount will remain privy to Jenkins and the Cubs' owner, Phil Wrigley, but it figures to settle around $115,000 to $125,000.

Looking back at his career, Jenkins admits to a certain satisfaction in his performances. "I guess I should be happy," he says. "After all, some very good pitchers never won twenty games even once. [Whitey Ford of the New York Yankees, one of the very best, registered just two over-twenty seasons]. But I still have goals. I'd like to win thirty some year, and with enough starts I think I can. I'm strong and I can pitch a lot of innings. That's most important, stamina. If I was the kind to tire easily, I don't think thirty would be possible. I'd have to get a lot of breaks, though."

The Cub batters can start by scoring more runs when Jenkins is pitching. In the past, they have displayed a disturbing habit of failing to score much for him. Indeed, he tied a major-league record in 1968 by losing five 1-0 games, and in 1971 he came out the loser in eight one-run decisions.

Where can Fergie stand improvement? "I'd like to cut down the number of home runs I give up," he says, "but pitching in Wrigley Field [which is tiny by comparison to many stadiums] doesn't help."

Finally, an anecdote just recently revealed goes a long way to show just how much determination and pride is stored within this hulking Canadian, a man whose mother has been blind since birth and whose father works as a chef in a Holiday Inn in Chatham.

Prior to the 1971 season, Fergie wrote down a list of objectives for the year, sealed the sheet in an envelope and taped it to the bottom of his locker shelf. After the season, he opened it for the Chicago press corps. It read: "A 26-9 record, stay healthy, don't get cheated at the plate and concentrate."

"Perhaps the most important was the good fortune in not losing my health," he says. "I had a little virus attack once, but I never had to miss a turn. Then I won the Cy Young Award, which really topped off my season. It wasn't even one of my goals, but who was I to say no?"

He came pretty close to all of his goals, close enough to become the best pitcher in the league in 1971. Whether he retains that edge over Seaver remains to be seen, but for one year, at least, he was on top of his world.

Dave McNally

He is sometimes called McLucky, but only by his friends and even then only when they are smiling.

What opposing batters and managers call the Baltimore Orioles' Dave McNally is something quite different, and most times hardly complimentary.

Why McLucky?

"Well, when he's pitching," says the Orioles' great third baseman, Brooks Robinson, "we always seem to get him five or six runs early in the game. Then we win it, like 6-5 or 7-6. The other pitchers on our staff just don't seem to get that kind of support from us, so they have to work hard to win the close ones. I guess Dave wakes up on the right side of the bed the day he's going to pitch, or he lives right, or something."

But Brooksie smiles when he speaks about this twenty-nine-year-old lefthander. McNally doesn't give away nearly that many runs, as his major-league career ERA of 3.00 will attest. And a pitcher has to be more than just a little McLucky to ring up four consecutive seasons of twenty victories or more, which is what this 5-11, 195-pounder has managed to do.

In addition, he has been the big winner on a pitching staff of consistent big winners, a staff clearly superior to, and more effective than, any other in either league; a staff which, in 1971, boasted four twenty-game winners in McNally, Jim Palmer, Mike Cuellar and Pat Dobson. It was the first time in fifty-one years than a team has had that many pitchers in the magic circle of twenty-plus.

In the past four years, McNally has won eighty-seven games while losing just thirty-one. He has won 135 in his major-league career, making himself the all-time Oriole winner. In three American League playoff series in the last four years, McNally has won three games, and in the three World Series played by Baltimore in that four-year span—the result of sweeping each playoff in three games— Dave has chalked up three more victories.

But perhaps there is something to this Mc-

Lucky business after all. It's possible to make a case for it.

Dave is not as fast as Jim Palmer, and therefore does not register the impressive strikeout totals of his mound mate. He does not have Cuellar's wide assortment of off-speed pitches, nor his stamina, and so he does not approach Mike's totals of complete games and innings worked. He does not have Dobson's natural speed and ability (Pat once won fourteen games for San Diego in a season when the club won only sixty-three), and so he has had to work harder to achieve his success.

"All Dave does really well is win," says Earl Weaver, his current manager. "He has all the pitches and the intelligence to know when to use them, and he's a hard worker with great determination. It's hard to say exactly what Dave does to win. I guess he blends all those things and comes out ahead. He wins, that's all."

That's all.

* * *

David Arthur McNally was born October 31, 1942, in Billings, Montana. The fact that he is a major-league pitcher today is a tribute to the American Legion's nationwide system of baseball leagues, since Central Catholic High in Billings offered only basketball as an interscholastic sport.

McNally made All-State in Montana as a basketball player, but he considered that just a wintertime diversion from baseball. "I liked basketball well enough," he says, "but I wouldn't have had any trouble picking baseball as my favorite. Basketball was fun, and it kept me in good physical condition."

So it was the summers, then, that Dave McNally looked forward to. In the three years he played Legion ball, he established a 40-6 record, with seasons of 10-2, 13-3 and 17-1, and four no-hitters in his final summer. It was enough to make a noise—even beyond Billings, Montana—and the noise brought the major-league scouts out in droves.

In the summer of 1960, having graduated from high school, McNally became eligible to sign a major-league contract. He was ready to become a professional, and he was eager for it.

But the presence of so many scouts confused him. "At first," he says, "it was a difficult choice. Lots of teams were interested in me, and lots of scouts became friends. I had to go through many offers, and then consider the men I might be disappointing."

Finally, the Orioles removed the difficulty—they offered Dave an $80,000 bonus for signing with them, and no other teams' proposal even came close.

So Dave became an Oriole.

He was sent to the Victoria Rosebuds of the Texas League, and at the start of the 1961 season, which was so full of anticipation, it seemed as though the team had made a costly error of judgment. After four appearances Dave had compiled an 0-3 record and had built an embarrassing 6.16 ERA.

The Orioles moved him to Appleton, Wisc., of the Three-I League, and while his record improved to 8-10 there, he had not yet shown any tendency to dominate batters with solid authority. His 4.18 ERA was not good, but the Orioles found some solace in his 155 strike-outs for just 140 innings of work.

In any case, he was deemed promising enough to warrant a promotion to the Orioles' Eastern League team in Elmira, N.Y. There, at last, he began to pitch to his potential, winging to a 15-11 record with such statistical highlights as a 3.08 ERA, 195 strikeouts in 196 innings and only sixty-seven earned runs allowed.

But working against him, suddenly, was the classic problem experienced by so many south-paws—lack of control. He led the league in walks, 115; in wild pitches, nineteen; and in hit-batsmen, eight.

The Orioles, carefully observing, acknowl-edged that Dave would probably soon join their major-league roster, but no one in the team's personnel department was ready to predict with unhesitating confidence that he would become a major-league superstar.

Then came September 26, 1962, and a lot of those people suddenly had cause to change their evaluation. McNally had been brought up to the major-league roster at the conclusion of his Eastern League season, and he was given a starting assignment against Kansas City. Baltimore was long since out of the running, and every major-league team not in pennant contention uses the end of the season to get an early look at some of the more promising farmhands who will be in spring training.

The result of the chance was a victory for McNally, but it was no ordinary win. It was not only a complete game, it was a two-hit shutout, and the Orioles were deeply impressed.

They had sufficient reason to be pleased with the prospects for his immediate major-league future, and they came to rely on him as a certain member of the starting rotation in 1963.

Dave McNally had reached the major leagues just two seasons after signing his pro contract, and he attributed his success to hard work.

"I had been working on my curve ball and slider," he says, "but at first I didn't have much luck. But near the end of the 'sixty-two season I began to find the plate. I grew confident in using the breaking pitches on two-strike counts. It started to fall into place for me. Then I had that two-hitter in my first major-league start, and it kind of put me over the top in confidence. I knew I had a chance to make the big team the following season, and that made me work all the harder. I didn't want to lose the opportunity. I was young, but I had had enough of the minor leagues."

The next three years were spent in the majors, but they were far from productive. McNally won twenty-seven and lost twenty-five during that period, his best performance an 11-5 mark in 1965, during which he came up with 116 strikeouts in 199 innings and a 2.85 ERA.

But then came the 1966 season, in which McNally emerged as a top-flight major-league pitcher and, not so coincidentally, the Orioles emerged as the finest team in major-league baseball.

In 1966, the Orioles had engineered a major trade, one which brought Cincinnati outfielder Frank Robinson to Baltimore. To acquire him, the Orioles surrendered pitchers Milt Pappas and Jack Baldschun and outfielder Dick Simpson to the Reds.

But in Robinson the Orioles had obtained a superstar. Frank was greatly upset by the trade, having spent ten years in Cincinnati, and he was riled at several remarks attributed to William DeWitt, owner of the Reds, at the time of the trade. "Frank is over the hill," said DeWitt. "We were lucky to unload him for three young, quality ballplayers."

Frank was so far over that hill that he proceeded to win the American League's Triple Crown—with a .316 batting average, forty-

nine home runs and 122 runs batted in—and
he was named the league's Most Valuable
Player for his performance, becoming the first
man in the history of the sport to have earned
that accolade in both leagues. (He had been
named the National League's Most Valuable
Player in 1961.)

Due mostly to his heroics, the Orioles won
the pennant by nine big games over the Minnesota Twins.

Baltimore's pitching in 1966 was superb,
and it was the very depth of the staff managed
by Hank Bauer that prevented any single
pitcher from dominating the statistics. "They
were all so good," Bauer once boasted, "that
I would just tell one of them to go out there
and win, and they would."

McNally built a 13-6 record and led the
staff's starters with his 3.17 ERA. But Palmer
led the staff in victories, with fifteen, and
others such as Wally Bunker (10-6), Steve
Barber (10-5), Stu Miller (9-4), Moe Drabowsky (6-0), Dick Hall (6-2) and Eddie
Watt (9-7) chipped in with enough victories
to make Baltimore a ninety-seven game winner.

"Until that season," says McNally, "I hadn't
had the kind of success people expected of me.
But afterwards, everybody figured I had made
it. We won so easily that the staff got lots of
publicity and credit, but I always felt the
weakness of the team was our pitching. I mean,

who couldn't win with the kind of hitting we got from guys like Brooksie and Frank and Boog Powell?"

The Orioles then embarked on a fantasy trip through the World Series, against the swift Los Angeles Dodgers. If the Dodgers had a weakness, it definitely was not in the pitching department.

That year's Los Angeles staff included the legendary Sandy Koufax (27-9, with a 1.73 ERA, 317 strikeouts and the Cy Young Award safely tucked away), along with such perennial winners as big Don Drysdale, Claude Osteen and a rookie named Don Sutton. Those three combined to win forty-two more games, while an efficient bullpen was paced by Phil Regan, who had enjoyed an incredible 14-1 season with a 1.62 ERA and an improbable twenty-one saves.

Weaknesses? Perhaps the Dodgers' main deficiency was a lack of power hitting. Their leading batter was outfielder Tommy Davis, not even a regular, who had a .313 average, and for power they relied on second baseman Jim Lefebvre, who hit twenty-four home runs, and leftfielder Lou Johnson, who added seventeen.

Clearly, the Dodgers did it with pitching and defense. They had won ninety-five games (to runner-up San Francisco's ninety-three), but never threatened to break open many of those games. A single, a stolen base and a ground ball amounted to much of the Los Angeles offense, and once Koufax or Drysdale had a one- or two-run lead, they were expected to hold it.

Weak hitting had become the trademark of those Dodger teams, as a Drysdale anecdote indicates.

He had been given permission to miss a night game, and when he was found the next morning, he was told Koufax had pitched a no-hitter.

"That so?" he drawled. "Did he win it?"

The other teams had the power, but they didn't have a chance of matching the Dodgers' pitching, and game after game one of the fielders would emerge as the subordinate star to the pitcher, having taken away a home run with a leaping catch or having denied a double with the bases loaded by diving for, and snaring, a liner down the third base line.

"They did it with mirrors," said Willie Mays, who was once again denied a World Series appearance as a member of the close-but-not-quite Giants. "I don't think there's a team in this league that couldn't out-hit the Dodgers, but with Koufax and Drysdale, anything they get is enough to win."

The Series opened in Los Angeles on October 5, 1966. It was Baltimore's first modern World Series appearance, for the current franchise had been granted to the city in 1954. There had been a Baltimore team in the major leagues, but its last year of big-league status was 1902.

McNally drew the honor of starting the Orioles' first modern Series game, and while he did not finish, Baltimore won the game. Dave did not get credit for the victory, however, since he was forced out with one down in the third inning, when a spell of wildness resulted in three straight walks. In came Drabowsky, the bullpen specialist, and for the next six and two-thirds innings he allowed the Dodgers just one hit while striking out eleven and walking no one.

The final score was 5-2, with Brooks and Frank, the Robinson terrors, each contributing a home run. The only Dodger run, predictably, was the result of a Lefebvre homer.

The next three games of the Series were also the last three games of the Series, as a stunned nation watched the Orioles register an astounding sweep of the heavily favored Dodgers.

Moreover, the Dodgers' humiliation was compounded by their failure to score even one run in any of the final three games.

First Palmer beat Koufax in the second game, 6-0. Then Bunker beat Osteen in the third, 1-0. Finally McNally, getting a chance to atone for his mild collapse in the opener, wrapped it up by tossing a 1-0 shutout at Drysdale, allowing just four hits.

Frank Robinson supplied the only run Mc-

Nally needed with a homer in the fourth inning, and the Dodgers' only threat was snuffed out by Paul Blair in centerfield, when he made a leaping catch at the fence in the eighth inning to deny Lefebvre a game-tying home run.

"Really, that was the only time I got scared all that game," Dave recalls. "I had my stuff working well, and the Dodgers were in a state of shock by then anyway. They could see what was happening and they just couldn't stop it. I know the feeling. We had it in 1969 against the Mets."

The defending World Series champions were more than just embarrassed, however. They were shaken, and through the 1971 season they had failed to win another pennant, not even a divisional crown.

Many people say that Koufax's decision to retire was triggered in part by the disappointment of that sweep. Others say that the 1966 World Series was the final test for his ailing left elbow, and when he saw he still had pain, he decided not to risk permanent injury.

In any case, when the Dodgers lost the superb athlete named Koufax, he left a gaping abyss in the pitching staff, and they have not been able to replace him properly since. Many have tried, pitchers such as Bill Singer and Don Sutton and Sandy Vance and Al Downing, but none of them have been able to come close to matching Koufax's dominance.

The Orioles, too, failed to capitalize on their 1966 victory, though for different reasons. In 1967 the Red Sox got hot. And in the same year McNally got started on a string of injuries and sore arms.

In spring training that year, pitching against the Twins, Dave reached back for a fastball and "felt something snap in my left shoulder." He left the game and was X-rayed by a doctor, who diagnosed the injury as a muscle tear. In the next few weeks, Dave made the usual rounds of doctors and specialists in athletic injuries without much to show in the way of results—or recovery.

What with the pain and the enforced idleness McNally struggled through the season with a 7-7 record, appearing in only twenty-four games and working a modest 119 innings. His ERA zoomed to 4.54, an indication of his hesitancy to come in with the fastball when he was in perilous situations during a game.

"It hurt, that's all," he says. "I couldn't throw with my usual speed, and that affected my rhythm. I would try to be cute with the batters rather than overpower them, and I lost my control." His strikeout total fell to a mere seventy, from 158 the previous season, and it appeared that, at the age of twenty-five, Dave McNally was destined for retirement.

"I was very depressed when the season ended," he admits. "The way my arm was still hurting, I didn't think I'd ever be able to pitch again. And the way I pitched that season, I knew the Orioles wouldn't want me if I didn't show any improvement. I really considered retiring. I knew I didn't want to go back to the minors and just hang on for another two or three years. That would have done me no good at all."

What Dave McNally needed was a miracle, and it was about to happen. But, as is the case with miracles, it began casually, in the clubhouse chatter that marks a professional team's daily atmosphere.

"We were talking with coach Billy Hunter one day near the end of the season," McNally remembers, "and as usual the subject of my sore arm came up. Hunter had been speaking to some doctors, and he had some of his own ideas. He suggested that I 'stretch out the tendons' by throwing easily at first, then harder, but under controlled circumstances and for the same amount of time each day.

"I wasn't very optimistic at first," he said, "and it just didn't sound convincing. But I decided to give it a try. I had nothing to lose and everything to gain. My career seemed to be headed down the drain anyway."

So when the season ended, a small group of Oriole players made plans for their winter of conditioning. The group included Jim Palmer, Curt Blefary, Tom Phoebus, Pete Richert and Brooks Robinson—along with McNally, the star pupil, and Hunter, their mentor.

They chose the Towson (Md.) YMCA, and after a body-building program of weight-lifting, running and exercising, McNally began to throw.

Toward the end of December he started letting it out, and he was surprised at the results. There was no further pain, and he seemed to have reacquired the snap and velocity his pitches required.

But McNally's troubles were still a long, long way from being over.

"When we got to spring training," he says, "I found out that Bauer was not counting on me for the starting rotation. He let me work out on my own, but he didn't feel he could use me if I was no better than the season before. I couldn't blame him. I hadn't been a very effective pitcher, and he had a team to worry about."

So McNally worked, and as the Florida sunshine soaked into his ailing left shoulder, he began to pitch with more authority. Loose was the word for his pitching near the end of the spring training period, and loose was the word coaches Hunter, George Bamberger and Vern Hoscheit used when they delivered daily reports to Bauer on Dave's rate of progress.

Finally Bamberger, who was the pitching coach, came up with his final decision. "The kid belongs in the rotation," he said. "As far as I can determine, he's as good as he ever was. Better, maybe, because he's worked so hard for it. He's smarter, and hungrier."

What followed was a performance of excellence which earned for Dave McNally the American League's Comeback of the Year Award in 1968. It was a storybook rally, one that moved even the hardened professionals on the team and the seasoned sportswriters throughout the league. The dimensions of his comeback were so far-reaching that he won the Comeback Award over two other pitchers —Ray Culp and Dick Ellsworth—who would have been automatic winners in almost any other year.

McNally won twenty-two games and lost only ten, appearing in 273 innings, starting thirty-five games, adding five shutouts, and fanning 202 batters. He was 14-2 over the second half of the season, a record that surpassed even that of the Detroit Tigers' Denny McLain, who was to win thirty-one games in 1968. McLain was 14-4 for the same second-half period.

The Orioles, however, failed to win the American League pennant, which went to Mc-Lain and his Tigers. But the team failure could in no way diminish the excitement and drama of McNally's return.

"I think he was the best pitcher in the league that year," said Bauer, who was relieved in mid-season by Earl Weaver. "It didn't matter how many games McLain won. Remember,

McLain got many more starts and he had a higher earned run average, gave up more hits and needed lots more support from his team. When Dave has control of his slider, he's the top pitcher in the league."

The slider, too, had returned in 1968. "I had had a pretty good slider when I started out in organized ball," McNally said, "but I lost it sometime during the 'sixty-seven season. I guess with all the arm trouble and the mental tension, I stopped trying to throw it. But in spring training that year, I was warming up with [catcher] Andy Etchebarren before an exhibition game with Atlanta.

"I was feeling pretty good, and so I motioned to Andy that I was going to throw a curve. Then I hollered: 'Watch this, I'm going to break off a slow one.' Well, I took something off the pitch and I shortened up on my delivery and the ball came in as a perfect slider. We tried the same pitch four or five times, and there it was. I had found the slider, and with that and the help of Bamberger and Hoscheit, I knew I had a chance to make the comeback."

Bamberger felt the rediscovery of Dave's slider was the key factor contributing to Dave's dramatic season. "He isn't the kind of pitcher who can get by with just a fastball and a curve. But when he can use the slider with control, he's outstanding."

Today McNally considers the 1968 season the turning point in his career. Without making himself sound corny, he freely admits that "I'm the luckiest guy in baseball. I was able to save a career that was more dead than alive."

Since then, of course, it has been all frills and trimming for McNally. He followed the 22-10 of 1968 with a 20-7 mark in 1969, the year the Orioles won the American League pennant following a three-game sweep of Minnesota in the divisional playoffs.

But it was also the year of the Miracle Mets, when the New York National League team, which had never finished higher than ninth in any of its seven years, shocked the baseball world by first winning its division title, then sweeping three games from the Atlanta Braves and finally, impossibly, winning the World Series from the powerful Orioles in just five games.

McNally, however, was superlative. On July 30, 1969, he set two American League records with his seventeenth consecutive victory, a streak that had begun on September 22 of the previous season.

Both records—for successive victories and for most consecutive wins at the start of a season—had belonged to Cleveland's Johnny Allen since 1937.

The streak ended August 3, when Minnesota's Rich Reese delivered a pinch-hit grand slam homer in the seventh inning to provide the Twins with a 5-2 victory.

During the seventeen-game string, McNally

pitched 190 innings and allowed just fifty-five earned runs, gave up forty-seven walks and struck out 123. He had ten complete games, including a one-hitter against the Twins spoiled by a Cesar Tovar single with one out in the ninth inning. Between July 11, 1968, and the day the Twins beat him, he had won twenty-nine of thirty-one verdicts, and that grew to thirty-one of thirty-five before he tailed off and dropped four in a row near the end of the 1969 season.

McNally's forty starts during the 1969 pennant season were just one shy of McLain's league-leading forty-one, and he was second on the staff to Cuellar in victories, innings pitched and strikeouts.

During the playoff with the Twins, McNally staged a magnificent second-game performance, pitching eleven innings and winning, 1-0, on a three-hitter—all of the hits coming before the fourth inning. He struck out eleven that day.

The World Series was a disheartening experience to the Orioles, who admit they were guilty of taking the Mets too lightly and believing that their improbable pennant victory had been a fluke.

"On the plane going home after we lost, I remember Brooksie saying that we should turn around and play them four more. He said we'd have won four straight with a different mental attitude, and I agreed. We all did. Losing to the Mets was our fault, not theirs."

McNally had lost once in the Series, despite otherwise stellar statistics of thirteen strikeouts in sixteen innings, five earned runs and only five walks. He lost the second game, 2-1, to Jerry Koosman (who had a perfect game for six innings), although he allowed only six hits and had a three-hitter for eight innings before losing the game to three ninth-inning singles.

But the Orioles, who had been prematurely crowned as overwhelming favorites, were disgraced in defeat, and it burned deeply. As McNally says, it became a turning point in the team's fortunes.

"The choice was up to us," he says. "We could have just kept thinking about the defeat, not concentrating on winning again, you know, and allow it to ruin our game. Or we could use it as a psychological weapon to get ourselves angry. We knew we had a great team— yes, better than the Mets—and we knew that losing the Series was our fault. We had to prove it was a mistake. It was our pride that was at stake, and it was even more important than the World Series money. We had to win back our self-esteem."

The next year provided more recovered pride than even the Orioles had dared to hope for. They waltzed to the American League pennant again, outlasting the hapless Twins in another three-game playoff sweep. But in 1970, the Mets failed to return to their fantastic world of miracles, and the Orioles drew the Cincinnati Reds as their World Series opponents.

This was the team that had come to be called The Big Red Machine. It had the slugging and the pitching, the speed and the defense, and it had made a joke out of the National League race. The Reds had won the Western Division flag by a whopping fourteen and a half games with their 102-60 record, and then had swept the Eastern Division champion Pittsburgh Pirates in three effortless games.

The Reds had dominated the better teams in its league, a certain sign of superiority. They had won thirteen of eighteen against second-place Los Angeles; fifteen of eighteen against Houston; thirteen of eighteen against Atlanta; nine of twelve against St. Louis; eight of twelve against Pittsburgh and eight of a dozen against the Mets.

Catcher Johnny Bench had hit 45 home runs with 148 RBI's and a .293 batting average. Third baseman Tony Perez had almost identical statistics, having slammed 40 home runs together with 129 RBI's and a .317 average. Pete Rose in the outfield was a .316 hitter, while first baseman Lee May had 34 homers and 94 RBI's and batted .253. Other slugging heroes included outfielder Bernie Carbo (21 homes, 63 RBI's, .310) and outfielder Bobby Tolan (16 homers, 80 RBI's, .316).

The pitchers had wondrous records; but with all that hitting, they almost had no choice. Jim Merritt was 20-12, Gary Nolan 18-7, Jim McGlothlin 14-10, Wayne Simpson 14-3, Clay Carroll 9-4, speedballing rookie Don Gullett 5-2.

Indeed, this was a super team, a team with more than superior strength at every position, a team with depth. But there was, surprisingly, a weakness. Cincinnati was not as good a team as the less-heralded but professionally brilliant Orioles.

Rose, the most talkative and competitive of the Reds and an annual batting championship contender, flatly predicted victory. But more importantly, he belittled the effect a pitcher such as McNally would have against the Big Red Machine.

"You just can't think of beating us with three pitchers [Dobson and not yet joined the Orioles], especially if two of them [McNally and Cuellar] are lefthanders. If we beat Jim Palmer in the first game, it will be the turning point of the Series.

"It would mean we'll be beating the guy Earl Weaver thinks has the best chance of beating us."

But Palmer did beat the Reds in the opener, 4-3, as he came up with a five-hitter. And then Cuellar, one of Rose's lefties, won the second game, 6-5. It was McNally's turn in the third game, the first time all season a team was attempting to beat the Reds twice in a row with two southpaws. And it was no contest.

Dave held the Reds to nine hits as the Orioles romped to a 9-3 victory. It was 3-0 in games now, and the cocky Reds were beginning to believe in the Baltimore mastery. It was a Series in which Brooks Robinson made three spectacular plays at third base, in each case depriving the Reds of run-scoring hits which, in all likelihood, would have won games.

It ended two games later, after the Reds stopped what had grown into a seventeen-game Baltimore winning streak (three in the Series, three in the playoffs and the final eleven games of the regular season).

"Brooks Robinson and those two [censored] lefties did it," said Rose. "Brooks could have played third base with a pair of pliers, and I don't think we saw two lefthanders as good as McNally and Cuellar all season."

The Orioles were now well in control of their destiny, and in 1971 Baltimore won yet another American League pennant as they again swept through the playoffs (making it nine straight in three years). This time the Oakland Athletics, not the Twins, were the foes, but the outcome was tediously similar. For the third year in a row, and the fourth in six, the Orioles were in the World Series.

The 1971 Series went to seven games, and

the Orioles somewhat disappointingly lost to the tenacious Pittsburgh Pirates. McNally won the opener and then lost the fifth game.

It had been another great season for Dave the Rave. He had compiled a 21-5 record with 224 innings pitched, a 2.89 ERA and six shutouts. His .808 winning percentage was the best in the major leagues. He won the opening game of the Oakland playoff series, beating Vida Blue, 5-3, with eighth-inning relief help from Eddie Watt. And then he won the Series opener, also 5-3, on a three-hitter.

"I had some control problems in the Series," he says. "I was missing the plate by two feet. But in the third inning of the opener it came back."

It had been a classic McLucky performance, for after he floundered on the mound and fell behind, 3-0, his teammates bailed him out. In the bottom of the second Frank Robinson clubbed a leadoff home run off the Pirates' nineteen-game winner, Dock Ellis. In the bottom of the third, Mark Belanger and Don Buford singled and outfielder Merv Rettunmund cracked Ellis for a three-run home run, making it 4-3. Buford added a solo homer in the fifth for the victory—McLucky's victory. It was the sixteenth in his last seventeen decisions.

But the Orioles' loss of the Series dampened, however slightly, McNally's 1971 performance. If he has his way, the Orioles will use this reversal, too, as motivation for future successes.

"It was just like the Mets' Series," he said after the Pirates won the seventh game. "We lost it because we made the mistakes. We deserved to lose, although we were the better team. Next season we'll show all over again just what a super team we have."

Indeed, it is a super team that lives in Baltimore. And it is a team fortunate to have as one of its pitchers the one they call McLucky.

Perhaps the Orioles have not considered it, but can they be super because they have McNally? And, if so, aren't they just a bit McLucky to have Dave McNally? After all, he is one of baseball's most outstanding lefties, McLucky or not.

Mickey Lolich

If baseball is still in command as the Great American Game (and despite the preenings and pronouncements of professional football, it is) then Mickey Lolich of the Detroit Tigers is not only good for the game but good for the American public at large.

And large, in this case, is an appropriate word. Mickey Lolich is a hefty man's hero, a chubby chowhound of sandwiches and pie, a pudgy pitcher who wins far more games than he loses and who caps each victory with another treat for his waistline.

But added weight does not bother Lolich, whose eating habits present a continual source of wonder and/or aggravation to his managers and coaches. In 1971, burdened with the sum of 220 pounds and anchored by the spare tire around his middle, Lolich was still enough of an athlete to lead the major leagues in victories, winning twenty-five games while losing only fourteen.

In addition, he was the major league leader in games started, forty-five; in innings pitched, 376; and in strikeouts, 308. His total of twenty-nine complete games fell just one short of the major league high of thirty registered by the Chicago Cubs' Ferguson Jenkins.

And all this was accomplished despite his bulky frame, despite the extra poundage most other athletes treat as a dread disease. Surely, Mickey Lolich would be even more effective with a trim body.

"Bunk," says Mickey Lolich. "I know how much I can weigh and not hurt my pitching. I believe the extra weight adds strength and stamina. It doesn't tire me at all. I find myself getting stronger in the late innings of a game, and I find my fastball picking up velocity because of the added momentum I get behind it. I might not look like the perfect athlete, but I'm happy with the way I perform, and I'm happy with my weight."

Lolich, thirty-one years old, enjoyed his best season in 1971. He came in a strong second to Oakland's Vida Blue in the Cy Young Award voting, and there were several players and thousands of fans who felt he should have won it, because they claimed Blue's victory was the result of his stupendous first-half per-

formance. When he tailed off in the second half of the season, Lolich was still pitching consistently well.

But Blue's acclaim was so widespread that Mickey toiled in near anonymity for most of the season. When Blue's run sputtered, fans were truly surprised to discover that Lolich had put together a record just as commendable.

On September 18, Mickey broke the Detroit strikeout record for a single season when he fanned Andy Etchebarren of the Baltimore Orioles. The 308 total he finished with was the highest since Sam McDowell, then of the Cleveland Indians, struck out 325 in 1965.

The 376 innings pitched represented the most in the American League in fifty-nine years, since Ed Walsh of the Chicago White Sox worked 393 innings.

But if 1971 was Lolich's best season, 1968 was his finest post-season. It was the last time the Tigers were involved in a World Series, and Mickey emerged as the clear-cut hero.

The lefthanded native of Portland, Oregon, complemented Denny McLain's thirty-one victories that season with seventeen of his own, and when the Tigers found themselves faced with the St. Louis Cardinals in baseball's annual autumn extravaganza, they naturally assumed that daffy Denny would be the man to lead them to ultimate victory.

It was not so. McLain was pelted with disturbing ease by the Cardinals, but they couldn't touch Mickey Lolich.

He won three of Detroit's four games in the Series, including the seventh-game clincher, and was a unanimous choice as the Most Valuable Player in the Series, an honor which brought with it the prize of a sports car donated by a national sports magazine. No one questioned whether Mickey would be able to fit his bulk in the car. No one joked about his car being equipped with an extra tire. Lolich had been far too impressive a pitcher. People were beginning to look with respect at his protruding pot.

Lolich won his three games, and they were all complete game efforts. He was strong and steady. His fastball and his curve were working to perfection, and he struck out twenty-one Cardinals in the twenty-seven innings. He walked only six men, allowed St. Louis one run in each of two games and finished with an imposing 1.67 earned run average.

In all, it was clearly the high point of his career, and it marked his entry into the upper strata of superstar pitchers. It had been a long time in coming, but Mickey Lolich was worth the wait.

Michael Stephen Lolich was born on September 12, 1940, and until he was ten years old he was a natural righthander. But a childhood injury to his right arm and shoulder forced him to choose between giving up athletics entirely or learning to use his left arm. It was really no choice at all. "Sports was my life," he says, "and I never even thought about giving up. It was kind of lucky that it happened so early, because I had plenty of time to adjust to being a lefty. At first it was difficult, but I was young enough to wait it out."

So Mickey became a lefty, and with the transition came the bugaboo of lefthanders— wildness, or lack of control.

"I found out that my left arm was much stronger for pitching," he recalls, "but I wasn't sure where the ball was going. When I threw righthanded, I didn't have the same speed or stuff but I had the control.

"I guess the biggest problem was learning to master the different pitches. But I was a kid and I didn't have too many pitches. By the time I grew, I was accustomed to being a lefty. But I always had the problem of wildness. When I let the pitches get away from me, I wasn't very effective."

There was, however, a great deal of interest in this young man on the part of several major-league scouts, and when he was eighteen he signed with the Tigers' farm system almost immediately upon graduating from high school.

For the first three years of his professional career, Lolich alternated his summers between Knoxville (Tenn.) of the Sally League and Durham (N. C.) of the Carolinas League. His first year, 1959, brought him a combined Knoxville-Durham record of 4-8, but he struck out 66 men in 104 innings. In 1960 he began to show the potential he possessed as a strikeout artist, when he registered 149 whiffs in 128 innings despite a Knoxville-Durham record of 5-11. His fastball was nothing less than a burning breeze exploding past the batters. But if he didn't strike them out, most times he walked them. He issued 107 passes that summer.

In 1961, Mickey's last Knoxville-Durham season, he had a 8-10 record, with 195 strikeouts in 174 innings. But again he was hurt by the absence of solid control as he walked 149 men. Yet the Tigers, who were in need of a strong-armed pitcher, began to thing of Lolich as the answer to their problem. They moved him to Denver of the American Association, a much more competitive league.

It was 1962, when Mickey was twenty-two years old, and perhaps the sudden jump in quality competition was too much. Whatever the circumstances, Mickey Lolich was a one-man disaster area in Denver.

He appeared in nine games but worked in only twelve innings. He was belted unmercifully, surrendering twenty-six hits and twenty-four runs, and that amounted to a woeful 16.50 ERA. The Tigers had to make a change, either in Mickey's surroundings or in their judgment.

They chose to move him, and it was off to his home town of Portland in the Pacific Coast League. The alteration of scenery worked a miracle. Mickey got untracked, found a reasonable degree of control and settled down to the job of pitching well enough to make the major leagues.

In twenty-three Portland appearances, he amassed a 10-9 record while pitching in 130 innings and striking out 138 hitters. His ERA was a sane 3.95, and he cut down the number of walks he allowed to a more than pleasing fifty-seven.

Now the Tigers made their decision. They brought Mickey up to the major-league roster to start the 1963 season, and he was so impressive in spring training that he stuck with the club. He appeared in thirty-three games, worked in 144 innings and added 103 strikeouts to his 5-9 record. His wildness, still a problem, was decreasing, and when the Tigers were forced to make room on their roster, they sent for Mickey.

"They told me I was going to Syracuse [in the International League], but they told me it was only a temporary move," he remembers. "They said it was the last time I'd see the minor leagues, and they told me the truth. I had to work on some pitches, and I had to get a lot of work. I couldn't do that with a team fighting for a pennant. I understood, and while it was a kind of disappointment, I believed

99

them when they said it would only be for a while."

It was to be for the remainder of the 1963 season, and Mickey got the necessary work he needed.

Chuck Dressen had taken over as manager of the Tigers in mid-season of 1963, and it was he who decided to send Mickey to Syracuse. "I knew the kid had a world of potential," he says. "He had speed and good stuff and we felt he could be a star. He needed some seasoning, some experience. That's all it was."

True to his word, Dressen brought Mickey to spring training with the Tigers in 1964 and he has remained with the major-league club ever since.

He had been a minor leaguer for the better part of five years, and now he was ready for the final promotion. All the experience and the seasoning and the pitching blended in Mickey Lolich, and he took the American League by surprise in 1964. He compiled an 18-9 record, the best percentage on the staff and just one game less than Dave Wickersham's team high of nineteen victories. He worked a yeoman 232 innings and led the team with 192 strike-outs. His 3.26 ERA was credible, and the Tigers knew they had found a winner.

"I guess I was as surprised as many people at the success I had that year," Mickey says. "I kept thinking all that season that this was the major leagues and these were major league hitters I was facing. For a while I couldn't believe I was winning and striking out so many of them. But that kind of experience sure builds your confidence. Pretty soon I got to thinking it wasn't all luck. That, for me, was the last major hurdle. I guess I had to start believing in myself."

The 1964 season established Lolich as a Detroit fixture. He registered a seven-game winning streak, longest for the team in years, and his six shutouts were the most by a Tiger pitcher since 1955. His future—and Detroit's —was bright, and they both faced 1965 with optimism.

In Mickey's case, it was not misplaced faith, for despite the team's faulure to win a pennant, Lolich had another record-breaking season. He built a 15-9 record and struck out 226 batters in 244 innings, the most strikeouts for Detroit since Hal Newhouser fanned 275 in 1946.

The seasons of 1966 and 1967, however, was not as spectacular, as the Tigers became a mediocre hitting team and Mickey fell to records of 14-14 and 14-13, respectively. But his strikeouts remained well-placed in league standings, and he had become acknowledged as one of the bright young pitching stars in major-league baseball.

However, another problem cropped up in 1967. Mickey became erratic. Indeed, it was a season of ludicrous extremes.

First he agonized through a ten-game losing streak, a run that saw him wait eighty-four days between victories. Then he turned around and won six straight, nine of his last ten. He was 9-3 in the second half of the season, with a 1.66 ERA, and he closed out the schedule with three consecutive shutouts and a skein of twenty-eight and two-thirds scoreless innings. In addition, he matched his club high of six shutouts.

The Tigers, meanwhile, were closing in on excellence. They had added solid players to their lineup, men such as Willie Horton and Dick McAuliffe and Don Wert and Mickey Stanley, and by spring training of 1968 many observers were predicting a pennant for Detroit. It was, they said, to be the Year of the Tiger. And they were right.

It was a well-balanced squad, complete with power and speed, depth and defense.

The pitching staff consisted of McLain, who captured the emotions of the nation with his conquest of the thirty-game barrier (he finished 31-6); Lolich, who was 17-9; the fastballing Earl Wilson, who had a 13-12 record; and young Joe Sparma, who contributed a 10-10 mark.

McLain led the league in games started (41), games completed (28), victories, winning percentage (.838), innings pitched (336) and opponents' at-bats (1,206). He totaled a club record of 280 strikeouts, and his 1.96

ERA was fourth-best in the American League while his strikeouts represented the league's second-highest total.

He was a unanimous Cy Young Award winner.

The Tigers won their pennant by a comfortable twelve games, and made ready to face the Cardinals in their first World Series since 1945.

It was a dramatic confrontation, for St. Louis had swept to its National League pennant with almost the same ease, finishing far ahead of the runner-up San Francisco Giants. But because of McLain's super year, the Tigers were rated as Series favorites.

McLain, naturally, drew the opening game assignment, and what a prospect that first game was! He was pitted against the incomparable Bob Gibson of the Cardinals, who had snapped through a 22-9 season.

McLain and the Tigers were favored—but Gibson and the Cardinals won. It was a 4-0 shutout for Bob, and the Cardinals held an important one-game lead.

It was a critical victory, for if Detroit could not even it up the next day—without its top pitcher—St. Louis would be in a position of authority. Having beaten the man who was thought to be the ace of the Detroit staff, the Cardinals were sky-high.

The second game assignment went to Mickey Lolich.

He was magnificent. In his first-ever World Series at-bat, he slammed a third-inning home run off Nelson Briles, but his heroics were on the mound, not at the plate.

Willie Horton provided him with a 1-0 lead in the second inning with a home run into left field seats, and Mickey's unique duplication of that feat made it 2-0 in the third. That would have been enough for Lolich to wrap it up, since he was to limit the Cardinals to six hits and only one run, but the Tigers flew into a batting frenzy that netted thirteen hits and an ultimate eight runs.

The lone St. Louis run was scored in the sixth, spoiling Mickey's bid for a shutout, and it was his own lapse that allowed it to happen. His old bugaboo, lack of control, caused him to walk Lou Brock, who then stole second, moved to third on a grounder by Curt Flood and scored on a single by Orlando Cepeda.

But Detroit had won, and the series was tied at one game each. Then disaster struck the Tigers, as first Wilson and then McLain suffered losses in the next two games and St. Louis was given a seemingly untouchable three-games-to-one advantage.

The fifth game was played in Detroit, and manager Mayo Smith went to Lolich. With the assignment went the burden of extending the Tigers' season, for a loss would have given the Series to St. Louis.

Mickey was shaky at first and quickly fell

behind, 3-0, in the first inning. He gave up a double to Brock, who scored on Flood's single, and then Cepeda cracked a homer, scoring Flood ahead of him, to provide the Cards with a lightning-quick lead.

But Lolich settled down after that and held St. Louis scoreless for the rest of the game; indeed, limiting the Cards to just six more hits in the final eight innings.

Meanwhile, Detroit was clawing back with frantic frenzy. Two triples, a single and a sacrifice fly in the bottom of the fourth provided two runs and cut the Cardinals' cushion to 3-2.

Then, in the seventh, the Tigers wrapped it up with a three-run outburst. And Mickey Lolich started it with a lead-off single to rightfield. That sent Briles to the clubhouse and brought in relief specialist Joe Hoerner, but he was no specialist that day. McAuliffe greeted him with a single and he then walked Mickey Stanley. With the bases loaded, Al Kaline's single brought in Lolich and McAuliffe, and Norm Cash finished it by singling home Stanley.

Detroit trailed now by a single game, and McLain evened it up the next day, finally showing the form that led him to his spectacular season. It was a 13-1 victory in which he allowed only nine harmless hits, and a grand-slam home run by Jim Northrup was all he needed. Northrup's slam came as the high point of a stunning ten-run third inning.

But McLain was finished for the Series, for even his supple arm and superman antics during the season could not get him ready to pitch on back-to-back days. Again it was up to Lolich, and manager Smith, for one, had no doubts as to the job Mickey would do.

"We'll win it," he said on the eve of the final game, in St. Louis. "With Lolich on the mound, we have all we need. The way he's been throwing the ball in this Series he's unbeatable. I don't think I've seen a better pitcher all season, unless it was McLain."

Mickey made his manager look like a clairvoyant, as he spun a five-hitter while locked in battle with the desperate Gibson. Detroit won, 4-1, completing the almost impossible task of surmounting a 3-1 games deficit, and only a ninth-inning home run by the Cardinals' Mike Shannon denied Lolich another shutout.

The Tigers had won their World Series—impossibly, incredibly—on back-to-back victories from their Big Two, Lolich and McLain. Those who knew the pair, and their growing dislike of each other, considered this to be the most ironic of twists.

Lolich had grown increasingly upset with McLain's attitude. Denny was a loner, but that did not prevent him from both criticizing the team and flouting manager Smith's authority. He carried on small grudge skirmishes with several of the Tigers, including Lolich.

Mickey felt this could only hurt the team in the long run, and he resented McLain's self-serving behavior. But he continued to maintain a veneer of harmony, if only to prevent further dissension from wracking and finally cracking the team.

But it boiled over in 1969, when both men were selected to represent the American League in the All-Star game. McLain, who flew his own small airplane, offered to take Mickey and his wife, Joyce, to Washington, D.C., for the game.

Mickey accepted, assuming the offer included a return flight to Detroit. But McLain, after being lifted for a pinch hitter after one inning, left immediately with his wife, Sharyn, for a two-day mini-vacation at his home in Lakeland, Florida.

The Loliches were stranded, and Mickey was incensed.

When a Detroit reporter named Pete Waldemeir saw Mickey on the commercial flight back to Detroit, and asked why he wasn't with McLain, the story exploded.

"McLain doesn't think about his friends or his teammates," Mickey charged. "All McLain thinks about is himself. He told me he was in a hurry to get down to Florida. When I asked him how we were supposed to get back to Detroit, all he said was 'that's tough, that's your problem.' I felt like I've been the victim of a crummy trick, and I don't like it. I don't care if you put it in the paper. I'm tired of this stuff. It's been going on long enough while everybody has been trying to hush it up."

Sure enough the story appeared in print— headlines—and it quite naturally made a stir. The feud was compounded when new information revealed that Denny was supposed to start the All-Star game but had been late in showing up at the stadium. Mayo Smith, was managed the All-Stars that year, had no choice but to give the starting nod to Mel Stottlemyre of the New York Yankees.

Indeed, McLain didn't arrive until twenty minutes after the game started—"I had a dentist appointment," he said—and he appeared not at all disturbed that he had missed such a pressing baseball appointment.

Detroit catcher Bill Freehan also was on the All-Star team, and he had warned Lolich the night before to make tentative airline reservations on a commercial flight back to Detroit— "because you just couldn't ever be sure of what McLain might do," he said.

The story charged up the Detroit fans, and most of them took Lolich's side. The first game after the All-Star break was at home against Kansas City. Mickey started and drew a wild ovation from the crowd, to which he responded with a four-hitter, striking out thirteen men and winning, 3-1.

It improved his record at that point to 14-2,

a glamor figure built with the help of a nine-game winning streak before the All-Star game. He was to win twelve of thirteen starts between May 7 and July 29.

The next night McLain was Detroit's pitcher, and he was roundly booed when he was introduced. But he shut out Kansas City, 3-0, for his fifteenth victory of the season. Freehan, commenting on the grudge between the two star pitchers, hoped it would ultimately benefit the team. "They're going out there trying to out-pitch each other," he said. "That just has to help the team if they keep it up."

In any case, it worked wonders for the two principal parties.

McLain finished the season with a 24-9 record while Mickey was 19-11. But the Tigers came in a close second to the Baltimore Orioles in the Eastern Division of the newly realigned American League, thus disqualifying themselves from the chance to defend their World Series championship.

When discussing Lolich today, one must consider the combative spirit he brings to the game. He slumped badly in 1970 and fell to a 14-19 record, but that served as the impetus for all he accomplished in 1971.

"After the 'seventy season," he said, "I actually started to hear people say I was washed up. Now that was silly. I was just thirty years old and I knew I was as good as ever; better, probably, because I was a smarter pitcher. I had lost some weight—the manager asked me to—and I felt that might have hurt my performance. I was getting tired.

"So I just went back to eating what I wanted to eat, and I put back some weight. It wasn't a big thing, but maybe it was mental. I just felt better . . . stronger . . . when we went back to spring training."

Others said Lolich's poor season in 1970 was the natural result of his sometimes weird antics off the field. While he is more serious and stable than McLain, he does have his idiosyncracies.

"Sure, I've been called crazy," he smiles, "and I've been called a kook. In baseball, if you don't conform to everything, if you don't do exactly what everybody else does, they call you flaky. But it doesn't really bother me. It's like my weight. Whatever is best for me, or whatever I really enjoy doing, I'll do. That is, as long as it doesn't hurt the team. I just like to do what I feel. I'm a guy who will try all sorts of things, challenging things.

"How else can I learn and experience? How would I ever have known the thrill of driving a race car if I never just got behind the wheel and did it myself? Someday I'm going to bail out of a plane to feel what parachutists feel, and one of these days I hope to drive a racing car at Indy."

Mickey's private life is, indeed, filled with

adventure. In 1969, he commuted from Detroit to his home in suburban Washington, Mich., some forty miles away, by motorcycle. And he would cut in and out of expressway traffic at seventy miles per hour.

When the team's general manager, Jim Campbell, suggested that this practice might be a bit dangerous, Mickey countered by saying he often took his daughter Kim, then three, for such rides.

Among his other thrill activities are stock car racing (he has driven at Daytona Beach, Florida, at 150 m.p.h.) and hydroplane racing (in which he has taken an unlimited class boat up to 95 m.p.h.).

But the most serious side of Mickey Lolich indicates a desire to ensure financial security. He made a series of sound income investments, and currently is a vice president of a chain of pizza parlors in the midwest as well as a sales representative for a manufacturer of snowmobiles. In January 1972 he staged snowmobile races, but he promised the Tigers he would not be a contestant, just a spectator.

After his superlative performance of 1971, Lolich headed into the 1972 campaign as one of the best pitchers in the major leagues, and as one of a few super lefties, a list which includes Vida Blue of Oakland, Dave McNally of Baltimore, Fritz Peterson of the Yankees, Wilbur Wood of the Chicago White Sox, Dave

Roberts of the San Diego Padres and Don Gullett of Cincinnati.

What more is there for Lolich to accomplish?

Predictably, he is not at all satisfied with what he has managed to do thus far. His major-league victory total stands at 141 games, and he wants to win "at least" 200. "But there's always something you do that you can do better," he says. "I'd like to have even better control, for instance, and I'd like to help the Tigers win a few more pennants and World Series. If I pitch as well as I know I can, there's no reason we shouldn't be pennant winners. We have a good, solid team."

So Mickey Lolich will continue to do things his way. He'll pitch every game as though it were the seventh game of a World Series. He'll speak his mind when he feels there is something which must be said. He'll strive to improve his already All-Star performances.

And he'll continue to eat.

He may not be the perfect athlete where appearance is concerned, but if the addition of twenty pounds or so could ensure a Lolich-type career, the nation's physical fitness program would be in big trouble.

"If I'm fat, so be it," says Mickey Lolich. "But I'm happy."

And the Detroit Tigers are happy too—happy with their paunchy pitcher from Portland.

Statistics

GEORGE THOMAS SEAVER

Year	Club	League	G	IP	W	L	Pct.	SO	BB	ERA
1966	Jacksonville	International	34	210	12	12	.500	188	66	3.13
1967	New York Mets	National	35	251	16	13	.552	170	78	2.76
1968	New York Mets	National	36	278	16	12	.571	205	48	2.20
1969	New York Mets	National	36	273	25	7	.781	208	82	2.21
1970	New York Mets	National	37	291	18	12	.600	283	83	2.81
1971	New York Mets	National	36	286	20	10	.667	289	61	1.76

G-games; IP-innings pitched; W-won; L-lost; Pct.-winning percentage; SO-strikeouts; BB-walks; ERA-earned run average.

FERGUSON ARTHUR JENKINS

Year	Club	League	G	IP	W	L	Pct.	SO	BB	ERA
1962	Miami	Florida State	11	65	7	2	.778	69	19	0.97
1962	Buffalo	International	3	13	1	1	.500	6	5	5.54
1963	Arkansas	International	4	10	0	1	.000	13	3	6.30
1963	Miami	Florida State	20	140	12	5	.706	135	59	3.41
1964	Chattanooga	Southern	21	139	10	6	.625	149	42	3.11
1964	Arkansas	Pacific Coast	11	57	5	5	.500	49	34	3.16
1965	Arkansas	Pacific Coast	32	122	8	6	.571	112	42	2.95
1965	Philadelphia	National	7	12	2	1	.667	10	2	2.25
1966	Phila.-Chicago	National	61	184	6	8	.429	150	52	3.33
1967	Chicago	National	38	289	20	13	.606	236	83	2.80
1968	Chicago	National	40	308	20	15	.571	260	65	2.63
1969	Chicago	National	43	311	21	15	.583	273	71	3.21
1970	Chicago	National	40	313	22	16	.579	274	60	3.39
1971	Chicago	National	39	325	24	13	.649	263	37	2.77

DAVID ARTHUR McNALLY

Year	Club	League	G	IP	W	L	Pct.	SO	BB	ERA
1961	Victoria	Texas	4	19	0	3	.000	19	18	6.16
1961	Fox Cities	I.I.I.	25	140	8	10	.444	155	96	4.18
1962	Elmira	Eastern	34	196	15	11	.577	195	115	3.08
1962	Baltimore	American	1	9	1	0	1.000	4	3	.000
1963	Baltimore	American	29	126	7	8	.467	78	55	4.57
1964	Baltimore	American	30	159	9	11	.450	88	51	3.68
1965	Baltimore	American	35	199	11	6	.647	116	73	2.85
1966	Baltimore	American	34	213	13	6	.684	158	64	3.17
1967	Baltimore	American	24	119	7	7	.500	70	39	4.54
1968	Baltimore	American	35	273	22	10	.688	202	55	1.95
1969	Baltimore	American	41	269	20	7	.741	166	84	3.21
1970	Baltimore	American	40	296	24	9	.727	185	78	3.22
1971	Baltimore	American	30	224	21	5	.808	91	58	2.89

MICHAEL STEPHEN LOLICH

Year	Club	League	G	IP	W	L	Pct.	SO	BB	ERA
1959	Knoxville	Sally	11	67	3	6	.333	42	53	2.55
1959	Durham	Carolina	9	37	1	2	.333	24	45	4.14
1960	Knoxville	Sally	4	15	0	1	.000	14	20	7.63
1960	Durham	Carolina	25	113	5	10	.333	135	87	4.06
1961	Knoxville	Sally	15	72	3	5	.375	93	76	5.10
1961	Durham	Carolina	18	102	5	5	.500	102	73	2.99
1962	Denver	American Assn.	9	12	0	4	.000	21	10	16.50
1962	Portland	Pacific Coast	23	130	10	9	.526	138	57	3.95
1963	Detroit	American	33	144	5	9	.357	103	56	3.56
1963	Syracuse	International	6	22	0	2	.000	21	10	2.45
1964	Detroit	American	44	232	18	9	.667	192	64	3.26
1965	Detroit	American	43	244	15	9	.625	226	72	3.43
1966	Detroit	American	40	204	14	14	.500	173	83	4.76
1967	Detroit	American	31	204	14	13	.519	174	56	3.04
1968	Detroit	American	39	220	17	9	.654	197	65	3.19
1969	Detroit	American	37	281	19	11	.633	271	122	3.14
1970	Detroit	American	40	273	14	19	.424	230	109	3.79
1971	Detroit	American	45	376	25	14	.641	308	92	2.92